If you're traveling to the beach, pack
your sunscreen. If you're heading for the
mountains, don't forget your climbing
boots. But if you're on the road to a deeper
understanding of Scripture, get the best
tour guide around: Lisa Harper. You
won't get lost. You'll be captivated by the
scenery. Most of all, you'll be glad you
made the journey.

MAX LUCADO

Lisa has a wonderful gift. She can plunge
into the depths of God's Word and extract
diamonds of wisdom and grace for every
hungry heart. I love to hear her speak but
never more so than when she is leading a
Bible study. This book will be like a breath
of fresh air to your soul.

SHEILA WALSH

Women of Faith speaker and author of
Extraordinary Faith

There are few people who have the true spiritual gift of teaching—breaking down deep spiritual truths into bite-sized portions that regular people, like me, can easily digest. Lisa Harper is an amazing Bible teacher and, more important, an authentic Christian. The nourishment you will receive from this or any book she writes will encourage and equip you to live a radical life for the Lord. Prepare to be blessed.

PRISCILLA SHIRER

Author of *He Speaks to Me: Preparing to Hear From God*

Lisa Harper will have you laughing and crying as she reveals the tenderness, passion, and joy of Christ. She is one of Christianity's bright and rising stars. So read her, spend time with her, and be blessed.

LAURIE BETH JONES

author of *Jesus, CEO*; *The Path*; and *The Four Elements of Success*

on the road with
Lisa Harper

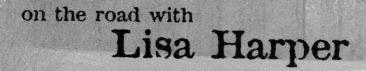

WHAT EVERY GIRL WANTS

*a portrait of perfect love & intimacy
in the Song of Solomon*

Tyndale House Publishers, Inc.
Carol Stream, Illinois

Visit Tyndale's exciting Web site at www.tyndale.com

TYNDALE and Tyndale's quill logo are registered trademarks of Tyndale House Publishers, Inc.

What Every Girl Wants

Copyright © 2006 by Lisa Harper. All rights reserved.

Cover photo copyright © by Photos.com. All rights reserved.

Front cover author photo copyright © 2004 by Kristin Barlowe, Inc. All rights reserved.

Front cover group photo taken by Victor Kore. Copyright © 2005 by Tyndale House Publishers, Inc.

Cover design by Jacqueline Noe; interior design by Beth Sparkman

Unless otherwise indicated, all Scripture quotations are from *The Holy Bible,* English Standard Version, copyright © 2001 by Crossway Bibles, a division of Good News Publishers. Used by permission. All rights reserved.

Scripture marked *The Message* is taken from *THE MESSAGE.* Copyright © 1993, 1994, 1995, 1996, 2000, 2001, 2002. Used by permission of NavPress Publishing Group.

ISBN-13: 978-1-4143-0278-2
ISBN-10: 1-4143-0278-9

Printed in the United States of America

12   11   10   09   08   07   06
7   6   5   4   3   2   1

I'm so thankful for my pastor, Scotty Smith, who consistently teaches that the Bible isn't merely a textbook—it's a supernatural love story. And I'm grateful for Lynn Husband, a gracious and wise Christian counselor, who has helped me recognize myself smack in the middle of that incredible, ongoing story.

Whoever brings blessing will be enriched, and one who waters will himself be watered. Proverbs 11:25

CONTENTS

How to Use the DVD

As you work your way through the book, you'll notice that certain questions have a DVD symbol next to them. Whenever you see this symbol, pop in the enclosed DVD, cue up the right chapter, hit play, and see what the book club has to say about this portion of Scripture.

You can watch as you go—one chapter at a time—or make some microwave popcorn and watch the whole thing while relaxing on the couch!

We really hope you enjoy "eavesdropping" on our conversations about God—and we hope they prompt some lively discussions with your friends, too!

Lisa

Introduction

I had to visit the Department of Motor Vehicles recently to get a new license, and it was almost as enjoyable as my last root canal. I don't know how the DMV manages to hire the grouchiest employees in the universe . . . maybe bad attitudes are applauded in their employee handbook.

Anyway, I was greeted by a unibrowed government "hostess"—who seemed like the type of person that eats small children for breakfast—and ordered to "take a number." After giving her a sheepish look, which I hope communicated my gratitude that she didn't wallop me, I timidly took B-151. Then I looked for the least grimy plastic chair to settle into among the other disgruntled citizens, whose posture belied the fact that they'd been camped out for quite some time.

My heart sank a little while later when that very same hostess announced that the computers were down. She paused dramatically for a moment and then declared (with a hint of masochistic delight) that they couldn't process our forms without the computers so we'd "just have to wait" until they could fix the technical glitch. Her declaration doomed us to several hours of bottom-numbing misery.

Many people—even "church" people—think studying the Bible is boring. That it provides the same sort of posterior

anesthesia as the DMV. Based on past experiences with bland teaching, someone else's bias, or simply a lack of exposure, a big chunk of our society caricatures the Bible as a dreary rulebook punctuated by "thees," "thous," and "begats." For inspiration, they would just as soon ponder the warning tags on their mattresses.

And that's the main reason the On the Road series was developed. This is the third book in a series designed to help people discover how interesting and relevant God's Word really is! We hope those who formerly balked at perusing divine literature will find themselves pleasantly surprised by the colorful imagery, captivating drama, and compelling promises. We also hope those who've been in a zillion Bible studies will be effectively reminded of what an amazing gift it is to interact with this life-changing text.

In *What Every Girl Wants*, we're going to visit a racy section of Scripture called the Song of Solomon or the Song of Songs. This biblical poetry makes soap opera plots pale by comparison. You might be shocked by the content of this Old Testament tale, and while you'll most certainly be encouraged, we're pretty sure you won't be bored!

Ultimately, we pray this supernatural story will help you have a clearer picture of who God is and how crazy He is about you.

1

Passionately Pursued

IF GOD IS THE PURSUER, THE AGELESS ROMANCER, THE
LOVER, THEN THERE HAS TO BE A BELOVED, ONE WHO IS
THE PURSUED. THIS IS OUR ROLE IN THE STORY.
                    John Eldredge, The Sacred Romance

Several months ago a friend lectured me about the
lack of direction in my romantic life. I think she
was trying to say a lack of momentum. Or the lack
of a pulse, since sometimes my dating life seems to
be barely breathing. Anyway, she strongly encouraged me to join an online dating service. Sigh.
I thought, *So, it's come to this.*

I know finding the love of your life via an
Internet connection is all the rage now—I've seen
the advertisements featuring cute couples gazing at

each other adoringly, so it obviously worked for them. But it still seems a little awkward to me. Not as desperate as advertising on the side of a bus, but awkward nonetheless.

My friend argued that the main reason I was hesitant about collaborating with a high-tech matchmaker was my pride. And since pride has certainly been my downfall before, I was convicted. I thought, *Maybe she's right. Maybe I should just get over myself and give it a try.* So I paid for a three-month membership.

That was four months ago and let's just say I should have followed my initial instincts. Not that there was anything *really* bad about the experience, but online dating just doesn't fit my personality. I like meeting people face-to-face over a mocha at Starbucks rather than hunched over a laptop, responding to an e-mail. I like watching new friends laugh, hearing the inflection in their voice, seeing the color of their eyes. And I didn't find that kind of personal connection on a computer screen. Dates just don't seem very *real* when they're dependent on electrical outlets.

did you know?

The Song of Songs is commonly known as one of the **Poetical Books,** which also include the books of Job, Psalms, Proverbs, and Ecclesiastes. Poetry does occur in several other Old Testament books (Moses' Song in Exodus 15, Deborah's Song in Judges 5, and Hannah's Song in 1 Samuel 2, to name a few), so the term **poetical book** is a bit of a misnomer. Thus, some Bible scholars prefer the terminology **Psalms and Wisdom** literature (and add the book of Lamentations to the grouping).[1]

I want a real love relationship with real intimacy. Something I believe *every* girl wants.

The Song of Songs (often referred to as "The Song of Solomon") is a colorful poem that stands out in biblical literature like white shoes after Labor Day. The lyrics are sometimes shockingly explicit—they seem more Danielle Steel than divine at first glance. Perhaps that's why it's missing from most Sunday school curriculums! And the most wonderfully scandalous thing about the Song of Songs is what it says about the kind of authentic intimacy we can have with God.

What mode of communication do you prefer to use with work or impersonal relationships: face-to-face, phone, or e-mail? Which do you prefer with friends and family? Explain your preference in each genre.

MORE INFO

"The Song of Songs" is a Hebrew idiom expressing the superlative, as in this is *the* song of all songs—the best, the most beautiful. That same Hebrew idiom is used in reference to the Holy-of-Holies (Exodus 26:33, *The Message*) and the King of kings and Lord of lords. It means the most excellent of all.[2]

What Did He Just Say?

I went to college at Troy State University in Troy, Alabama, for my junior and senior years. The area was quite different from where I grew up in central Florida. Among other things, Troy wasn't what you'd call metropolitan. It was a small, laid-back Southern town where people were quick to extend hospitality but pretty slow about everything else. Needless to say, the local music scene wasn't exactly cutting edge. Therefore, when I went home on school breaks, I tried to pay attention to new radio hits so I could help my friends back in L.A.—lower Alabama—keep up with contemporary playlists.

During one school break, I heard a new pop song from a tiny musician with huge hair named Prince. Like Cher and Ghandi, he's one of those single-name people—although he went through a season where he wanted to be known as a symbol, not a name. Anyway, I thought his song was really cool, so I memorized a few lines in order to teach it to my sorority sisters back in Troy. It went something like this: *She wore a red, spherical dress. The kind you find in a secondhand store.* Or so I thought.

Within days of returning to school, I'd told most of the girls about this "great, new song by Prince" and shared the catchy lyrics. So we were proud to strut our stuff when the song finally made it to the Troy playlists. We pranced out onto the fraternity dance floor en masse and began to belt out, "She wore a red, spherical dress. . . ." until someone approached us and asked, "What were you just singing?" To which one of us, probably silly me, repeated the lyrics with panache. But I was quickly exposed as a musical moron when he explained that the words of the song were actually: *She wore a raspberry beret.*

What's your most embarrassing example of mangling a song lyric?

How Should We Peruse This Poem?

Before we start sifting through Solomon's Song, I need to warn you that some of the lyrics are difficult to understand. Therefore, we're going to take

just a moment to consider the best way to "hear"— or interpret—the language of this book.

There are numerous interpretive styles, and Bible scholars still debate which one is the best. I don't want to get so technical as to encourage mental field trips, but I do want to briefly explain the various methods in order to justify the lens through which we'll look at the Song.

Historically, four or five different approaches have been popular when it comes to interpreting this book.[3] The first is purely *allegorical*, which is basically an extended metaphor. I don't think this approach is valid, mainly because it essentially ignores the historicity (the actual historical details—real people and places) of the text.

Another interpretative style is that this book was written as a *drama*, casting Solomon as an ancient Shakespeare on marital relations. I don't favor this method either because I think it marginalizes the text into a summer paperback. Something to thumb through for entertainment.

The most common method is the *natural* or *literal* interpretation, which argues that this Old Testament book is simply a poem, communicating the hopes, desires, disappointments, and reconciliation of two young lovers. This approach synopsizes the Song of Songs into a marriage primer of sorts. Something to encourage love and sexuality, like God's version of the Kama Sutra.

Additional interpretive methods for the Song of Songs include the *mythical* or *cultic* approach, which links this Old

MORE INFO

A famous rabbinic sage—Saadia—once commented: "Know, my brother, that you will find great differences in interpretation of the Song of Songs. In truth they differ because the Song of Songs resembles locks to which the keys have been lost."[4]

Testament book to the erotic literature of ancient fertility cults. And finally, there's the *typological* approach, which is derived from the Greek word *typos,* meaning a pattern or what is produced from a pattern. This style recognizes the validity of the Old Testament account, and then finds a parallel link—or pattern—in the New Testament.

Whew! That's a lot of information, isn't it? However, we're not going to use any of the above approaches in their strictest sense in this book, and I'll explain why in just a minute.

Who Wrote This Wild Stuff?

It's commonly assumed that Solomon—King David's wealthy and wise Old Testament son, who wrote most of Proverbs and possibly Ecclesiastes—was the author of the Song of Songs, although some biblical scholars debate this assumption. Evidently, there are several linguistic issues that cast doubt on sole Solomonic authorship. But none is so compelling that Solomon can be irrevocably dismissed as the author. And theologians do agree that Solomon was the central male character in this love song. So maybe he wrote this poem, or part of it, or maybe it was written in his honor. Either way, it chronicles an amazing tenth-century (BC) romance between Solomon and his "favorite" wife.[5]

Just in case you flinched when reading that last sentence, it's important to remember that Solomon

MORE INFO

The Bible is a progressive revelation, inspired by God and written by the Holy Spirit over a span of around 1,400 years through the pens of some forty or so different authors. When authorship of a particular section of Scripture is indefinite, theologians encourage readers to focus on the content of the text versus who was God's "scribe."

lived during a time period when polygamy was the norm, especially for the rulers and chieftains. You'd probably be hard-pressed to find someone who embraces polygamy among your current circle of friends—unless you live in certain parts of Utah—but having more than one wife wasn't anything to write home about in this ancient era (although Solomon's harem might've prompted a postcard or two because he was such an enthusiastic wife collector). Scripture says he had seven hundred wives, as well as three hundred concubines (1 Kings 11:3). That's a lot of estrogen at one address! The Bible also tells us it got Solomon in a heap of trouble:

> **MORE INFO**
>
> For a detailed biography covering the colorful personal life and illustrious accomplishments of King Solomon, read 1 Kings 2–11 or 2 Chronicles 1–9.

> *For when Solomon was old his wives turned away his heart after other gods, and his heart was not wholly true to the LORD his God, as was the heart of David his father.* 1 Kings 11:4

But please don't assume he was some lecherous millionaire, because for most of his life he was a godly man and a good king. Furthermore, it's a widely held belief (especially in the Jewish rabbinic tradition) that the Song was written when Solomon was a young man and celebrates the true "love of his life," or at least, the first girl who really captured his heart.[6]

Who was the first person you developed a crush on in elementary school? Did it ever sprout into a relationship?

What's Up with You?

Now by this point, some of you are probably asking yourself, *Why is she writing a book on the Song of Songs?* Which is a legitimate question. Why would a single girl like me, with a checkered dating past—basically a Bridget Jones among Bible thumpers—choose to write a book about the most romantic, erotically charged section of Scripture? The argument could be made that I'm like someone on the Atkins diet who can't have donuts, but gets a weird charge out of pressing her nose to the window at the Krispy Kreme place and watching them go through the glazing machine.

> **MORE INFO**
>
> Some Bible scholars think the Song of Songs is not actually one poem, but an anthology, or collection, of love poetry.[7] Others argue for the structural unity and see the poetic divisions as distinctive sections similar to a prologue, individual "chapters," and an epilogue.[8]

But I prefer to think of myself as kind of a Bible tour guide, and my purpose in writing about the Song is to introduce people to the encouraging truths found in this amazing poem! Because the treasures in Solomon's words are for *everyone*—men, women, single, married, widowed, black, white, red, or purple—who yearns to connect with God through an intimate relationship with Jesus. And while it would be ignorant of me to claim that romance and marriage aren't the central themes in the Song, I do think a more inclusive yet still theologically responsible way to interpret this book is a *Christocentric*, or Christ-centered approach—looking at key passages and considering how they *illustrate* our walk of faith.

Because at some level, this eye-popping poetry points to our relationship with God. Jesus Himself said so in the Gospel of Luke:

That very day two of them were going to a village named Emmaus, about seven miles from Jerusalem, and they were talking with each other about all these things that had happened. While they were talking and discussing together, Jesus himself drew near and went with them. But their eyes were kept from recognizing him. And he said to them, "What is this conversation that you are holding with each other as you walk?" And they stood still, looking sad. Then one of them, named Cleopas, answered him, "Are you the only visitor to Jerusalem who does not know the things that have happened there in these days?" And he said to them, "What things?" And they said to him, "Concerning Jesus of Nazareth, a man who was a prophet mighty in deed and word before God and all the people, and how our chief priests and rulers delivered him up to be condemned to death, and crucified him. But we had hoped that he was the one to redeem Israel. Yes, and besides all this, it is now the third day since these things happened. Moreover, some women of our company amazed us. They were at the tomb early in the morning, and when they did not find his body, they came back saying that they had even seen a vision of angels, who said that he was alive. Some of those who were with us went to the tomb and found it just as the women had said, but him they did not see." And he said to them, "O foolish ones, and slow of heart to believe all that the prophets have spoken! Was it not necessary that the Christ should suffer these things and enter into his glory?" And beginning with Moses and all the Prophets, he interpreted to them in all the Scriptures the things concerning himself.

Luke 24:13-27

These two guys are walking home from the very first Easter week in Jerusalem, kicking at pebbles in the road because they don't really understand what happened. They're depressed that the political-religious system conspired against a "good man." And that this man, named Jesus, died an unfair death. But then Jesus Himself—whom they don't yet recognize—walks up beside them and asks, in effect, "Why the long faces, guys?" They look at Him in disbelief like, "You've got to be kidding!" because they're shocked that this stranger doesn't know what just transpired in Jerusalem. Everybody is talking about it. It's front-page news in *Israel Today*. Has this man been living under a rock or something? So they explain, probably with exasperation or condescension, the events that have taken place.

Jesus listens to their entire spiel, then says something like this—and I picture Him with a hint of a smile here—"Don't you remember? We studied this in Old Testament 101; the prophets told us this would happen!" He continues by patiently reviewing God's merciful plan to redeem mankind through His death and resurrection, which they have just witnessed. Starting the lesson in Genesis and continuing through the prophets, *he interpreted to them in all the Scriptures the things concerning himself.* In other words, Jesus takes these two bewildered men on a comprehensive Old Testa-

ment tour in order to say, "All of this points to the Messiah . . . it's all about Me!"

Read Isaiah 53. What do you think this Old Testament passage says about Jesus?

Dr. John Murray, a respected theologian and professor, made this observation regarding Christ and the Song:

> *I also think that in terms of the biblical analogy the Song could be used to illustrate the relation to Christ and His church. The marriage bond is used in Scripture as a pattern of Christ and the church. If the Song portrays marital love and relationship on the highest levels of exercise and devotion, then surely it may be used to exemplify what is transcendently true in the bond that exists between Christ and the church.*[9]

Another well-respected theologian and professor, Dr. Tremper Longman III, says this about the application of the Song:

> *Throughout the Bible relationship with God is described by the metaphor of marriage. As with any metaphor, the reader must observe a proper reticence in terms of pressing the analogy. Nonetheless, from the Song we learn about the emotional intensity, intimacy, and exclusivity of our relationship with the God of the universe.*[10]

The exclamation point of these few paragraphs is that this candid love poem isn't *just* for

FAST FACT
Martin Luther blazed the trail for the **Christological** teaching style, which essentially means to highlight Christ—or the promise of Christ—when expositing Old and New Testament Scriptures.

married people! Whether you got roses from a sweetheart this past Valentine's Day, feel called to singleness, have celebrated your fiftieth wedding anniversary, are struggling with divorce or the death of a spouse, or you're connecting with someone via an e-mail romance, the Song of Songs is for you!

did you know?

The Song of Songs is part of the third section of the Hebrew Bible called the **Kethubim**, which means "the Writings." The Writings are a pretty diverse collection, including the prophetic book of Daniel; the historical books of Chronicles, Ezra, and Nehemiah; the poetry of Job, Psalms, and Proverbs; and finally a section called the Five Scrolls, which includes Ruth, Lamentations, Ecclesiastes, Esther, and the Song of Songs.

These five books were very familiar in Hebrew culture because they were read out loud at major Jewish festivals in much the same way we might emphasize the spiritual significance of Easter with a passion play or dramatize the birth of Christ with people in bathrobes pretending to be shepherds. The book of Ruth was read out loud at the Feast of Weeks, celebrating the barley harvest in late May (Ruth 2–3; this was fifty days after Passover; Pentecost happened then, too). Lamentations was read out loud in late July to commemorate—or **lament**—the anniversary of the destruction of Jerusalem in 587 BC (2 Kings 25:1-12). Ecclesiastes was read at the Feast of Tabernacles in late September or early October, when they built and decorated elaborate outdoor shelters—or **tabernacles**—commemorating their forefathers' time in the wilderness (Leviticus 23:33-44). Esther was read at the Feast of Purim in late February, which celebrates the Jews' deliverance from the genocidal intent of Haman—he's the obnoxious guy who was hung on the gallows he had his servants build for Mordecai, Esther's guardian (Esther 9:16-22). And our focus, the Song of Songs, was read at Passover, which is considered the most significant of the Hebrew festivals as it celebrates their deliverance from Egypt (Exodus 12:12-14).[11]

In light of the "Did You Know?" fact about the place of the Song of Songs in Hebrew culture, why do you think the book was chosen by Jewish religious leaders to be read out loud at Passover?

Dying for a Kiss

Let him kiss me with the kisses of his mouth!

Song of Solomon 1:2

My first kiss with the last man I dated was sweet. We'd been together for a while and were committed to getting to know each other well before sharing physical affection. So when the moment finally arrived, I was more than ready! We were standing outside on a starry night, after sharing a great meal in a romantic restaurant, and he began to tease me about how long he'd been waiting for this particular peck. His voice was warm, his eyes were twinkling, and he looked oh, so handsome in his suit. So when he leaned toward me, I responded with a grin, closed my eyes, and kissed him back!

Jeanne Guyon was a fiery Frenchwoman who got into a lot of trouble because of one particular kiss recorded in Scripture. She wrote a commentary on the Song of Songs (among various other biblical manuscripts) in the seventeenth century. And she had the courage to write that the lyrics in Solomon's Song could be applied to all believers, not just Solomon and his bride. She was one of the first commentary authors to observe that this ancient poem illustrates the love relationship between God and us. She wrote that the *kisses of his mouth* referred to a spiritual union: "a real, permanent, and lasting experience of God's nature. The kiss is the union of God's spirit to your spirit."[12] Which makes my parking lot smooch pale by comparison!

As a result of Jeanne Guyon's Christocentric, yet controversial, interpretation, some of the most influential churchmen in France (including Archbishop Bossuet, a man referred to as "the Catholic Church's answer to Martin Luther") gathered to investigate her writings. Historical accounts reveal that these powerful men of the cloth were none too pleased by Madame Guyon's style.[13] Of course, most of them had taken the vow of celibacy, so it's no surprise a book about erotic poetry wasn't their cup of tea! For Jeanne Guyon to dare imply that we could experience passion in our relationship with God infuriated those religious leaders. So much so that she was eventually sent to prison in the notorious Bastille for her "blasphemy."

You know, that's what got Jesus in major trouble, too. For teaching that we could actually experience intimacy with our heavenly Father. That we could have a loving *relationship* with God instead of just mind-numbing religion.

DVD **Have you ever felt "kissed" by God? If so, describe the circumstances around His most recent show of affection.**

2

Feeling Pretty Enough

LET US LOOK AT OURSELVES, IF WE CAN BEAR TO, AND SEE
WHAT IS BECOMING OF US. FIRST, WE MUST FACE THAT
UNEXPECTED REVELATION, THE STRIPTEASE OF OUR
HUMANISM.   *Jean-Paul Sartre*

In the first chapter of his book, *The Journey of Desire*, John Eldredge talks about the times in our lives, that we would return to if we could. Moments that were full of love and joy. I imagine Christmas mornings from my childhood. Or one of those close-to-perfect summer days, sweetened with good friends and cold watermelon. Eldredge laments that treasured moments like these pass and the mental photographs fade, leaving us yearning for them once more.

**Read Song of Songs chapter 1 in the New
Living Translation or *The Message* and
synopsize this chapter in your own words.**

DVD **Can you remember a time in your life that
seemed so perfect you wish you could
recapture it?**

> *Then God said, "Let us make man in our image,
> after our likeness. And let them have dominion
> over the fish of the sea and over the birds of the
> heavens and over the livestock and over all
> the earth and over every creeping thing
> that creeps on the earth." So God created
> man in his own image, in the image of
> God he created him; male and female he
> created them.*
>
> Genesis 1:26-27

MORE INFO

Aseity: (noun), existence orig-
inating from and having no
source other than itself.[1] The
aseity of God refers to His
all-sufficiency, His absolute
completion, His lack of need,
and His perfect unity with
Himself. Saint Augustine illus-
trated this when he said,
"Only the Christian God is a
community unto Himself."
Therefore, God didn't create
us because He was lonely.

God is an "Us." He existed in perfect
community with Himself in the Garden
of Eden. And the reason we yearn to
feel deep connection is because we
were created in His image. Adam and
Eve experienced perfect relationship with this
wonderful, Trinitarian God in Eden, and we too
were imprinted for perfect intimacy. But the
memory of that garden romance has paled and
we've grown all too accustomed to a *lack* of
intimacy.

**What characteristics must be present in a
relationship before you consider it to be
"intimate"?**

I watched a middle-aged couple interact in a restaurant recently. A Cracker Barrel to be exact. They made it through their salads, entrées, and desserts without saying more than a few words to each other. I don't think they were fighting, because they didn't look mad. They looked sad. And I'm pretty sure it *wasn't* because they wished they'd ordered the chicken 'n' dumplings instead of the meatloaf! I think they were married; they were both wearing wedding rings and they had that "we've been together forever" appearance. But they sure didn't look *happily* married. They looked like they had simply given up on connecting with one another. They looked like they were just wearily going through the motions of relationship. I was tempted to buy them something sweet from the gift shop because that always cheers me up.

There's a scene in the movie *The Shawshank Redemption* where Morgan Freeman—playing a wise old convict who's been incarcerated for a long time—says, "At first, these walls, you hate them. They make you crazy. After a while you get used to 'em, don't notice 'em anymore. Then comes the day you realize you need them."

Some of us have become willingly imprisoned in lukewarm relationships. We've settled for little scraps of attention and affection, instead of insisting on the deep intimacy we were created for. And we've grown so used to being misunderstood, ignored, and poorly loved, that we generally prefer

> **MORE INFO**
>
> *Ontological equality* is the belief that the three members of the Trinity are equal in "being" or "value," yet their roles are diverse. God the Father *plans* redemption; God the Son *effects* redemption; and God the Spirit *applies* redemption. The high priestly prayer in John 17 is an interesting passage to read if you want to ponder the ontological equality of God further.

the safety of superficiality to the risk of being known. It's much easier that way. That's probably why the lyrics in the Song of Songs are such an affront to the average Christian. They remind us of what we're *supposed* to long for.

 **Read Psalm 63. Which of the action words that David wrote in this Psalm—*thirsting, fainting, looking, being satisfied,* or *clinging*—best defines your walk with God right now? Describe a season when you felt absolutely satisfied by God's love.**

Is Hard-to-Get Holy?

Let him kiss me with the kisses of his mouth!
For your love is better than wine;
your anointing oils are fragrant;
your name is oil poured out;
therefore virgins love you.
Draw me after you; let us run.
The king has brought me into his chambers.

Song of Solomon 1:2-4

This girl definitely isn't playing hard to get, because right from the beginning of their relationship she breathlessly declares her desire for his affection. I guess she didn't read *The Rules* because she's coming across as way too needy, don't you think? I mean, *Good night! She should at least try to act cool. What if he's just not that into her?* Surely she sabotaged her position with him when she revealed that all the other girls think he's cute too, *right*?

Finally, she flings subtlety out the window when she voices her desire to check out the Little League trophies in his "chambers," or his *bedroom*! Feigning aloofness is obviously not one of her attributes.

Are you more comfortable being pursued in a romantic situation, or being the pursuer? How about in friendships; would you describe yourself as more of an *initiator* or a *responder*?

If we were being frank, many of us would describe this girl—Solomon's soon-to-be-bride—as a bit too eager. Conservative sentiments encourage women to manage their expectations. We're told to disguise our longing for love so we won't scare away potential suitors. And humanly speaking, I guess there's some truth to that. I've met more than a few men who seem genetically programmed to *hunt* for a mate. It would obviously behoove me to entice guys like that with indifference—so their inner caveman would be compelled to pursue me. Maybe I should use the money I've saved by abandoning the online dating game and invest in camouflage.

But God isn't a regular human Romeo. We don't have to be coy to allure Him. On the contrary, our Creator encourages us to express our love for Him. Remember how Jesus welcomed the messy exuberance of children, much to the disciples' dismay?

> *And they were bringing children to him that he might touch them, and the disciples rebuked them.*

NOTES

But when Jesus saw it, he was indignant and said to them, "Let the children come to me; do not hinder them, for to such belongs the kingdom of God. Truly, I say to you, whoever does not receive the kingdom of God like a child shall not enter it." And he took them in his arms and blessed them, laying his hands on them. Mark 10:13-16

And remember how God's favorite head of state, King David, danced a heartfelt jig in appreciation of Jehovah's faithfulness to Israel?

And David danced before the LORD with all his might. And David was wearing a linen ephod. So David and all the house of Israel brought up the ark of the LORD with shouting and with the sound of the horn. 2 Samuel 6:14-15

David's wife, Michal, got mad because of his Saturday-Night-Fever moves. She didn't think his behavior was appropriate for royalty. Yet Scripture defines David as "a man after [God's] own heart" (1 Samuel 13:14), so our heavenly Father obviously appreciated David's animated boogie.

Then, who could forget the way Jesus applauded a sinful woman's public display of affection when she washed His feet with her tears, dried them with her hair, and then poured designer perfume all over them?

One of the Pharisees asked him to eat with him, and he went into the Pharisee's house and took his place at the table. And behold, a woman of the city, who was a sinner, when she learned that he was

*reclining at table in the Pharisee's house, brought
an alabaster flask of ointment, and standing
behind him at his feet, weeping, she began to wet
his feet with her tears and wiped them with the
hair of her head and kissed his feet and anointed
them with the ointment. Now when the Pharisee
who had invited him saw this, he said to himself, "If
this man were a prophet, he would have known who
and what sort of woman this is who is touching him,
for she is a sinner." And Jesus answering said to
him, "Simon, I have something to say to you." And
he answered, "Say it, Teacher."*

*"A certain moneylender had two debtors. One
owed five hundred denarii, and the other fifty.
When they could not pay, he cancelled the debt of
both. Now which of them will love him more?"
Simon answered, "The one, I suppose, for whom he
cancelled the larger debt." And he said to him,
"You have judged rightly." Then turning toward
the woman he said to Simon, "Do you see this
woman? I entered your house; you gave me no
water for my feet, but she has wet my feet with her
tears and wiped them with her hair. You gave me
no kiss, but from the time I came in she has not
ceased to kiss my feet. You did not anoint my head
with oil, but she has anointed my feet with ointment. Therefore I tell you, her sins, which are
many, are forgiven—for she loved much. But he
who is forgiven little, loves little."*   Luke 7:36-47

Jesus chastised this important religious leader
for choosing propriety over passion. And He
blessed a wanton woman's overt fondness for Him.

God doesn't demand a façade of restraint or religious decorum. He celebrates our eagerness. He is delighted by our desire for Him. He is very much *into us.*

Have you—or someone you know—read the recent book *He's Just Not That Into You?* **If so, what was your/their impression of the romantic advice in it?**

One Hot, Horsey Girl

If you do not know,
O most beautiful among women,
follow in the tracks of the flock,
and pasture your young goats
beside the shepherds' tents.
I compare you, my love,
to a mare among Pharaoh's chariots.
Your cheeks are lovely with ornaments,
your neck with strings of jewels.
Behold, you are beautiful, my love;
behold, you are beautiful;
your eyes are doves. Song of Solomon 1:8-10, 15

did you know?

Solomon uses equine words—like **mare** or in some translations, **my filly**—ten times in this romantic book. In light of his impressive literal stable—Solomon's reputed to have owned thousands of horses—and the fact that horse ownership was an elite pursuit, using **filly** instead of **sweetheart** makes sense. Although most women now would be insulted to be compared to a horse, it's obvious that Solomon wasn't using the term in a derogatory sense!

Solomon, who history asserts is the bridegroom in this poetry, doesn't act like a stereotypical boyfriend here, either. He lays all his romantic cards on the table from the get-go and woos this chick, "Shulamith," with gusto. (See "Did You Know?" on page 29.)

When's the last time someone sincerely complimented you? How did you respond?

Several years ago, I read a novel called *Stones from the River*, by a gifted storyteller. The drama unfolds in a small German village and chronicles the life of a woman named Trudi, who is a dwarf. The story is heartbreaking from the beginning; Trudi's mom suffers from mental illness and has a complete breakdown when Trudi is born. She dies when Trudi is four years old, leaving the little girl to assume that if she hadn't been born "little," her mother wouldn't have gone crazy and died.

Of course, Trudi has to deal with the inevitable taunts and stares of others throughout her childhood and young adulthood. She experiences the ugliness of human prejudice and therefore doesn't believe she'll ever be loved because of her appearance. But then, during World War II, a man named Max befriends Trudi and falls in love with her intelligence and fiery, independent spirit. Yet when he confesses his love for her, she thinks he's mocking her. After all the years of cruelty and discrimination, she simply can't believe that an average-sized man could actually love her.

My favorite scene in the book takes place when Max and Trudi are lying beside a river in the springtime. He's telling her how much he loves her and how beautiful she is, while tracing the outline of her miniature body from her head to her toes. Max finally convinces Trudi of his affection. That beauty is in the eye of the beholder.

I think most women can identify with Trudi at some level, because very few of us really think we're beautiful. Regardless of what the mirror reveals, we typically think we fall far short of the standard. Thin, blonde women daydream about chest enhancement. Short brunettes shop for those elusive "comfortable" stilettos. Being satisfied with the appearance God gave us is rare, and genuine gratitude for His handi-work is even more uncommon.

Recently a kind acquaintance made a point of telling me that I had pretty legs after she saw me wearing a skirt. I was flustered because I was in a chubby season and didn't think any part of my body was all that attractive. It was difficult to say thank you instead of making a self-effacing comment like, "I think you probably need glasses."

We often sully God's love with that same kind of insecurity. When He whispers that we are fair, we roll the eyes of our hearts and say, "You must need glasses, God. I'm not pretty at all."

One of the greatest truths we can glean from this ancient, colorful prose is that God *is* wearing glasses. Rose-colored glasses tinted with the blood of Christ. And through those glasses our Beholder finds us very beautiful.

Read Psalm 139. What's your favorite verse in this passage? How would you paraphrase verses 13-14?

3

A Rooftop Romancer

He brought me to the banqueting house,
and his banner over me was love.
Sustain me with raisins;
refresh me with apples,
for I am sick with love.
His left hand is under my head,
and his right hand embraces me!
I adjure you, O daughters of Jerusalem,
by the gazelles or the does of the field,
that you not stir up or awaken love until it pleases.

Song of Solomon 2:4–7

A few years ago I went out with a man who was a serious romantic. On several occasions, he cooked my favorite meal—and didn't let me lift a finger to help—then served it outside under the stars. He took me horseback riding and dismounted in order to point out his favorite wildflower, then picked one and handed it to me. And let me tell you, he was one cute cowboy. Just like the girl in this Old Testament poem, I was all but "sick with love" the first time I saw him in leather chaps!

Even though we lived in the same town, he wrote me letters in longhand. We'd typically see each other in person at least once or twice between when he mailed the letter and when I received it, so it wasn't very practical. It's not like he was off at war with no other means of communication. Plus, we talked on the phone all the time. But he said he still liked the idea of me walking to the mailbox and getting a letter with his thoughts in writing.

Once, when I met him at his place for a date, I noticed little pieces of dark chocolate everywhere. They were on the mantle, on the windowsills, in the guest bathroom, and on the furniture. Everywhere I looked, I saw Hershey's Special Dark. It was as if the sugar fairies had visited during the night and scattered their wares. I thought maybe he'd had a craving for something sweet and then sort of absentmindedly scattered it around the house. You know how messy bachelors can be. But then I thought, *That still doesn't make sense, because he doesn't like dark chocolate.*

So I asked him why his home was littered with Hershey's. He grinned mischievously. I alleged, "I didn't think you liked dark chocolate." He replied with a wink, "I don't." Then it dawned on me that he was courting me with candy. I said demurely,

"Did you put all that chocolate all over the house just for me?" And his eyes lit up with a smile when he shrugged and said, "I thought you might get a little hungry before we ate dinner."

All this *and* he was a committed Christian man, who excelled in business, enjoyed the outdoors, quoted poetry, knew how to cook, and didn't have a weird relationship with his mother.

Dreamy, huh? So why didn't I walk down an aisle toward him wearing a white dress with something borrowed and something blue? Well, it turns out he was only a reconnaissance romantic. Although he talked about marriage, introduced me to his friends and family, and pondered adopting children, he wasn't ready to "go public" with our relationship. I found that out when he complained about me using the term *dating* with some mutual friends. I didn't even use his name; it was just a general reference to our situation.

But still, wouldn't you assume that when someone called you several times a day, *and* invited you to eat with him at nice restaurants at least once a week, *and* drove through a tornado to see you in another state, *and* mused about what to christen your hypothetical children, *and* said you were "God's gift to him," *and* said that he'd wait "as long as it took" for you to believe he was "the one," that you were "dating"? Yeah, me too.

I was more than a little disappointed by his sudden reversal. If you look close enough, you can still see the imprint of his foot on my heart. This guy wined and dined me for months; then, when I actually started to fall for it, he recanted. It was

NOTES

like junior high school, when you held hands with your "boyfriend" in the dark safety of the movie theater, but as soon as the credits rolled and the lights went up, you raced back to your girlfriends while your preteen lothario swaggered over to join his pals. Both acting like the other had a full-body rash.

It takes a real man to treat a woman the same way in public—in full view of the entire world—that he treats her in private.

Read Song of Songs 2:1-7 in the New Living Translation or *The Message* and synopsize these verses in your own words.

Have you ever been treated poorly in public by someone who seemed nice in private? If so, how did his or her emotional discrepancy affect your relationship? (The circumstances don't have to be romantic; you can get "jilted" by an insensitive friend or family member.)

A High Profile Relationship

He brought me to the banqueting house,
and his banner over me was love.

Song of Solomon 2:4

Chapter 1 records the love language of Solomon and his would-be bride, Shulamith, in a private setting, a dark theater, if you will. But their sweet talk continues in the very public atmosphere of the banquet house in chapter 2.[1] They've essentially gone from a clandestine booth in an off-the-beaten-path eatery to a mall—on the day after Thanksgiving. They're bound to run into tons of people they know. Friends and strangers are sure to see them holding hands. It's going to be obvious to *everyone* that they're dating.

And to make his sentiments perfectly clear, just in case anyone missed the fact that they are making goo-goo eyes at each other and wearing matching T-shirts, Solomon starts waving a big banner with "I love this woman" painted on it. Unlike my insincere Romeo, this man's behavior declares, "I want everyone to know how much I love you, baby. I want to shout it from the rooftops!"

What's the most radical romantic gesture— planning a birthday scavenger hunt, writing an original poem, or renting a billboard—someone's ever done for you? How did you respond to his overture?

Like Solomon in this love story, God doesn't attempt to conceal or disguise His affection for us.

did you know?

The silver-tongued bridegroom in the Song of Songs first uses the word **Shulamith** (in the original Hebrew text) as a term of endearment for his bride in 6:13. Shulamith is preceded in the original Hebrew text by an article, "the," which functions to introduce a vocative case, meaning a noun or name, directly addressed. Most scholars agree the name Shulamith is the feminine version of Solomon's name, like Robert and Roberta. Solomon's name is derived from the Hebrew word **shalom** (commonly used as a greeting, but also meaning "general wellness").[2]

Scripture never records Him being aloof in front of people after whispering sweet nothings in the dark. He doesn't try to act cool and jam His hands in His pockets when others see you out in public together. God has been up front about His pursuit of us from the beginning of biblical history.

He advertised His bond with the Israelites via a supernatural blimp in the wilderness. It was a cloud by day that morphed into a ball of fire at night (Exodus 13:17-22). Not exactly subtle. And His death on a cross wasn't what you'd call under-stated, either. Remember what the men asked Jesus on the Emmaus Road?

> *Are you the only one in Jerusalem who hasn't*
> *heard what's happened during the last few days?*
>   Luke 24:18 (*The Message*)

In other words, "Good night! Haven't you been watching CNN or reading the newspaper? *Every-body's* been talking about how this guy named Jesus was killed at Golgotha!" Our Messiah's death on the cross was a very public execution. His match-less valentine gift made headlines all over the ancient world.

God is not secretive about His love for us. He's been declaring it in infinite ways since the begin-ning of time. He shouts His affections for us from the rooftop of the universe!

What's the most meaningful expression of affection you've received recently (not neces-sarily a *romantic* expression)?

Be Still My Heart

Sustain me with raisins;
refresh me with apples,
for I am sick with love.   Song of Solomon 2:5

I saw a movie starring hunky Brad Pitt recently. There's a scene about halfway through the film where Brad is talking with his wife on the phone. They're in the middle of an argument and a breakup seems inevitable. Thus, Brad becomes nostalgic; he tells his wife that contemplating the end of their relationship makes him think about the beginning. He goes on to describe what he thought the very first time he saw her. He gets this tender, faraway look on his ruggedly handsome face, and pauses. Then he smiles softly and says, "I thought . . . I thought you looked like Christmas morning." At that, all the women in the theater breathed a collective, "Awwww" and clasped our hands to our chests! His expression and words were so sweet that we were mesmerized for a moment. Communally crushed-out.

> **MORE INFO**
>
> A more accurate translation of the words *banqueting house* (Song of Songs 2:4) would be "the house of wine." Idiomatically, "the house of wine" could be a vineyard or a place where wine is manufactured, consumed, or stored.[3] So in modern context, our drama would take place in Sonoma, California, or better yet, an Italian vineyard in Tuscany!

But our group infatuation pales next to the response of Solomon's fiancée. She's so captivated by his profession of love that she literally swoons. Her face flushes and she puts a hand over her trembling heart. She starts feeling woozy, so she folds into a chair to keep from passing out. Then she asks for something to eat because the ardor has left her famished. And I like that about her. I can't identify with scrawny girls who complain about losing their appetite!

Moreover, this Old Testament girl is very specific about her choice of snacks. She requests *raisins* and *apples*, fruits that Hebrew scholars say were viewed as sensual stimulants or symbols in the Ancient Near East.[4] Kind of the way we think about oysters. Personally, I'd rather eat Styrofoam, but some folks rave about the aphrodisiac effect of oysters. Like Viagra on the halfshell. And while I question the erotic influence of a slimy bivalve, I'd still have to suppress a smile if I overheard a starry-eyed couple order them at dinner. I wonder if Solomon grinned when his girlfriend placed her order for *passion* fruit!

Then, in much the same way that Solomon went for broke with the whole *banner* escapade, Shulamith ventures past the point of no romantic return with her next comment:

> **MORE INFO**
>
> The Hebrew word that's translated *raisins* in verse 5 occurs only three other times in the Old Testament (2 Samuel 6:19; Isaiah 16:7; and Hosea 3:1). Raisins were almost always associated with religious festivals. Sometimes they were even shaped into triangular *cakes* to represent female genitalia.[5]

Do you think the people closest to you would describe you as *reserved* or *demonstrative*? Which do you use most often to communicate affection: *words*, *deeds* (cooking a special meal, buying a gift, etc.), or *physical touch*?

> *His left hand is under my head,*
> *and his right hand embraces me!*
>
> Song of Solomon 2:6

Dr. Craig Glickman, a former professor of ancient languages who is considered an authority on the Song of Songs, explains that this expression occurred in other poetry of that era and says it depicts sexual intimacy.[6] It was as if she was saying, "I want to lie down beside you, with both of your arms around me. One hand on the small of my back and one behind my head." A modern-day poet named John Mayer used similar phrasing in the beautiful but explicit song "Your Body Is a Wonderland," which earned him a Grammy for best pop vocal performance in 2003:

Something 'bout the way the hair falls
in your face,
I love the shape you take when crawling towards
the pillowcase,
You tell me where to go and,
Though I might leave to find it,
I'll never let your head hit the bed,
Without my hand behind it.[7]

did you know?

The term **Ancient Near East** generally pertains to the early civilizations that predate classical antiquity. It was a region that roughly corresponds to what we call the Middle East. As such, it is a term widely employed in the fields of Near Eastern archaeology, ancient history, and Egyptology. The Ancient Near East is generally understood as encompassing Mesopotamia (modern Iraq and Syria), Persia (Iran), Egypt, the Levant (Israel, Jordan, Lebanon, Syria, and Palestinian Authority), and Anatolia (Turkey). Some users of the term would extend its application into the Caucasus region, modern Afghanistan, Minoan and Mycenaean Greece, and other peripheral areas.[8]

I can't imagine too many Bible commentaries that reference radio hits, but I couldn't help noticing the parallel lyrics. And I couldn't help gloating that this almost-three-thousand-year-old text is so relevant that the language is echoed by a twenty-something rock star! Yet another example of why Scripture should *never* be described as boring.

What's the most beautiful depiction of love you've ever seen in a movie, heard in a song, or read in a book (other than the Bible)?

The Parameters of Passion

Before you raise your eyebrows in disapproval and dismiss Solomon and his lady's conversation as *tawdry*, remember that this poetry is divine literature. Just as much a part of the Holy Writ as Paul's New Testament letters. Furthermore, God never condemns sensuality in Scripture. He is not a member of Victorian society who frowns at uncovered ankles. He actually applauds sexuality—more on that later—as long as it's in a relationship He's sanctified.

One of my close friends has a son who's in the throes of puberty. Some of his behavior is humorous. Like when he douses himself with enough cologne to fumigate their house. Or the way he's become devoted to primping; he can't pass a mirror without flexing or raking his fingers through his hair. And when he watches a couple kiss on television now, instead of saying, "Ew, gross!" like he used to do, he observes them intently as if trying to memorize a technique!

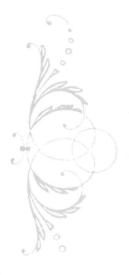

But his newfound attraction to young women is nothing to laugh at. Especially when little girls in big-girl bodies pursue him and promise sexual favors. So his mom asked his youth pastor to have a frank talk with him. And the pastor used a great analogy. He told this precious preteen boy that sex is like fire. It's beautiful to watch in a fireplace, where it gives comfort and warmth. But it's also dangerous. A fire raging out of control isn't enjoyable or comforting—it's scary. It has the ability to destroy everything in its path. Fire needs to be contained to be pleasurable.

In the same way, sex can be immensely pleasurable when enjoyed within the "fireplace" of a monogamous marriage. But when experienced outside the boundaries of a man and wife, it becomes destructive. It has the ability to burn the hearts of every person in its path.

That's why Shulamith takes a deep breath, puts up her hand, and says, "Okay, we'd better pour some cold water on this hot topic!"

> *I adjure you, O daughters of Jerusalem,*
> *by the gazelles or the does of the field,*
> *that you not stir up or awaken love*
> *until it pleases.* Song of Solomon 2:7

The fact that Shulamith and Solomon are sexually attracted to each other is *a good thing.* However, she also knows that Jehovah won't bless their lovemaking until they're married. So she's determined to restrain the flames until then. And she doesn't presume it's

MORE INFO

The word *adjure*—some translations use the word *charge*, instead—is a common Hebrew word. The form used here (Song of Solomon 2:7) means to "beg urgently" rather than the idea of taking an oath.[9]

going to be easy to keep the lid on their libido, either. She takes extra precaution by asking her friends, the *daughters of Jerusalem*, to help hold her accountable.

Contrary to the unbiblical philosophy of some stodgy church members, it doesn't honor God to act like you've had your sensuality surgically removed. You don't need to be a wallflower in the bedroom because you teach a Bible study. *Purity and prudishness are not the same thing!* God created us with a sex drive. He doesn't remove our hormones when He redeems us, He just teaches us when to set them free!

 Read 1 John 1:9. What's your opinion about the idea of a "second virginity" for those people who had sex outside of marriage, but because of their relationship with God are now committed to abstinence until they're married?

4

A Huge Portion of Happy

WE'RE EASTER PEOPLE LIVING IN A GOOD FRIDAY WORLD.
Barbara Johnson

My good friend Emily is a beautiful blonde. And she's so sweet that I'm able to overlook her high metabolism. We were walking in the park recently, talking about relationships and how love has a way of making people lighthearted. I asked her about the silliest thing she'd ever done while falling in love with her husband, Jason, and she started to giggle.

She said they were at a retreat when they were both students at Stanford, not too long after they'd made the transition from friendship to dating. The retreat director had launched the weekend by encouraging everyone to go outside and spend some time reflecting on God's goodness. So Jason went off by himself to focus. As he pondered the freedom that Christ affords us, he decided to express himself by rolling down a hill like he had done as a little boy. When he came to a stop, he spotted Emily above and called up to her, "As you wish," a catchphrase from one of their favorite movies, *The Princess Bride.*

Emily said her heart surged with affection over Jason's playful behavior. She was so enchanted that she impulsively hurled herself to the ground and began to emulate his barrel roll with equal enthusiasm. All the while laughingly proclaiming that same movie line, "As you wish . . . as you wish . . . as you wish."

But her downhill course was a bit steeper and she picked up more speed than she'd planned. She said she didn't expect to roll right past him into some trees!

Emily's delightful display of affection reminds me of the next verse in the Song of Solomon:

> *The voice of my beloved!*
> *Behold he comes,*
> *leaping over the mountains,*
> *bounding over the hills.*   Song of Solomon 2:8

Leap
to spring through the air from one point or position to another; jump[1]

Much like Emily's tumble toward Jason, the imagery of Solomon sprinting up and down hills toward his beloved is precious. He's so taken with Shulamith that he's literally leaping!

Read Song of Songs 2:8-15 in The New Living Translation or *The Message* and synopsize these verses in your own words.

If you feel comfortable doing so, describe your first brush with true love. What's the silliest thing you've ever done because of love?

Remember, we're not perusing these lines in the Song of Songs the same way we would the lyrics of Elizabeth Barrett Browning or John Keats. This story isn't merely a poem. Solomon's Song is inspired by the Creator of the universe, the supreme "poet." He punctuates His verse with stars and uses thunder for exclamation points. Thus, these words aren't just about a boy and a girl. At a certain level, they elucidate the kind of relationship we can have with God. They echo His extraordinary affection.

Furthermore, this Old Testament poem isn't the only biblical portrayal of God running toward us.

> *There was a man who had two sons. And the younger of them said to his father, "Father, give me the share of property that is coming to me." And he divided his property between them. Not many days later, the younger son gathered all he had and took a journey into a far country, and there he squandered his property in reckless living. And when he had spent everything, a severe famine arose in that country, and he began to be in need. So he went and hired himself out to one of the citizens of that country, who sent him into his fields to feed pigs. And he was longing to be fed with the pods that the pigs ate, and no one gave him anything.*
>
> *But when he came to himself, he said, "How many of my father's hired servants have more than enough bread, but I perish here with hunger! I will*

*arise and go to my father, and I will say to him,
'Father, I have sinned against heaven and before
you. I am no longer worthy to be called your son.
Treat me as one of your hired servants.'*

*And he arose and came to his father. But while
he was still a long way off, his father saw him and
felt compassion, and ran and embraced him and
kissed him.*   Luke 15:11-20

The Prodigal Son is one of the most familiar
stories in the Bible. Jesus narrates a colorful tale
about how one rebellious young man coerces his dad
into giving him access to his trust fund early. Then
he spends it all in JerusaVegas—on cards and call
girls—and ends up living in a homeless shelter.
There he finally recognizes the stupidity of his hard-
partying lifestyle and decides to head back home.

He's broke, humiliated, and repentant. On the
drive home, he ponders what his dad's reaction will
be to his homecoming. He thinks he'll receive a furi-
ous lecture and exile in the garage apartment at best,
complete rejection at the worst. Therefore, he's taken
by complete surprise when he turns the corner into
his old neighborhood and sees his dad jogging
toward him in pajamas. He's stunned speechless
when his father pulls him into a teary bear hug.

The prodigal son represents humanity—we are
all sinners, wired to wander and wallow in selfishness. But like the dad in Christ's parable, our heavenly Father's love is bigger than our rebellion.
This beautiful portrait in Luke reveals the same
thing about God that Solomon's Song does: that
He runs toward us.

Compare the story of this sinful son in Luke 15:11-32 to the story of the sinful woman we read about in Luke 7:36-50. What do these two people have in common? What do you think is the relationship between repentance and intimacy with the Lord?

Knocking Down the "Door" Metaphor

You might be wondering why we're spending so much time focusing on how demonstrative God is. We've already established His unbridled zeal in Chapter 2. We covered His very public declaration of love in Chapter 3. And now here we are fixating on the anthropomorphic image of God racing through suburbia in a bathrobe.

So what's the big deal about God being an affection exhibitionist?

I guess it's my feeble literary attempt to balance perception. Because in my opinion, God has been cast as standoffish for far too long. He's often caricaturized as a Darth Vader kind of deity, unwilling to feel compassion for humanity, but quick to vaporize anyone who might provoke Him. Or He's painted as some shallow Santa/Daddy/Wizard of Oz figure who can't connect on a deep emotional level but still gives great presents if you're a "good" girl or boy.

Which caricature was the most common in your spiritual upbringing—God as a distant *Darth Vader*, or God as an unconnected, overly permissive *Santa/Daddy*?

Anthropo-morphic ascribing human form or attributes to a being or thing not human, especially to a deity[2]

There's a key verse in the New Testament, as familiar to most churchgoers as the Prodigal Son story, that has been manipulated to perpetuate the myth of God's standoffish nature. It's found in the biblical caboose of Revelation:

> *Behold, I stand at the door and knock. If anyone hears my voice and opens the door, I will come in to him and eat with him, and he with me.*
>
> Revelation 3:20

At first glance these words portray a different image than the one of God madly in love with His bride. He seems more polite than passionate here. And thus, many preachers and teachers describe God as a "gentleman." Essentially someone who stands on the welcome mat of our life, just waiting to be invited inside. Kind of like a shy schoolboy peddling candy bars. Or a salesman hoping we'll turn off the vacuum cleaner so we can hear him ringing the doorbell.

But the common interpretation of God as a gentleman is woefully deficient. First of all, if God is such a timid chap with good etiquette, then what in the world happened to Paul on his Damascus road trip (Acts 9:1-19)? Did God simply forget His manners when He blinded Paul? God certainly didn't stand outside the "door" of Paul's heart, waiting for him to get a clue and invite Him in for tea. He blew the hinges off!

Secondly, the book of Revelation, where this oft-twisted "gentleman" verse is found, is a series of prophetic visions that God gave the apostle John when he was exiled on a Greek island. And the context of this dream is the apathy of the first-century church. Jesus was knocking on the door of this lethargic spiritual community to see if anyone would wake up and repent. He was interrupting their religious sleepwalking.

He was *not* wringing His holy hands on the porch of humanity. God isn't reticent or passive when it comes to us. He is an expressive bridegroom, actively pursuing His beloved and running toward repentant sinners.

What are some other scriptural examples of God *pursuing* individuals? Describe ways in which He's pursued you recently.

I Can't Take My Eyes off of You

A long time ago I went to a hairstylist who really shouldn't have been allowed near scissors, much less coloring chemicals. Due to the way she ruined several women's coiffures, her client list had dwindled, but I felt so sorry for her that I kept going back, against my better judgment. So, for almost a year, I looked like I was wearing a red wig made from roadkill fur.

During that same horrible hair season, I was dating a very kind man. One night at dinner, after a particularly bad trim, I sensed him staring at me. I glanced up and found myself looking into eyes full of adoration. Somehow, in spite of my crimson shag, he found me appealing.

Shulamith has already confessed that she is different from the other girls Solomon could have courted (Song of Solomon 1:5-6). She is dark brown, her tan betraying the fact that she has to work outside in a vineyard pulling weeds and hoeing rocks under a scorching sun. She isn't some Old Testament debutante who lives a life of luxury. She doesn't get her nails done, she doesn't drive a hot car, and she doesn't carry around one of those little Paris Hilton dogs. She is a blue-collar babe, like Cinderella *before* the glass slipper.

With Shulamith's common labor vocation and looks more exotic than classical, some men undoubtedly walked right past her. Like romantic lemmings, they followed the rest of the male masses hunting conventional feminine beauty, the type airbrushed on magazine covers and smiling in toothpaste commercials. But Solomon doesn't pay attention to popular opinion. He doesn't watch *Jerusalem's Top Model* or have a subscription to the *Orthodox Man's Quarterly*. He thinks Shulamith is absolutely gorgeous—calluses and all—and can't take his eyes off her.

> *My beloved is like a gazelle*
> *or a young stag.*
> *Behold, there he stands*
> *behind our wall,*
> *gazing through the windows,*
> *looking through the lattice.*
>
> Song of Solomon 2:9

Even more so than Solomon—or my charitable former beau—Jesus gazes at us with unmerited favor. Blemishes and all.

Is there a person in your life who consistently overlooks your shortcomings in a way that reminds you of Jesus?

A Walk to Remember

I think taking a trip with one other person is an intimate endeavor. And I'm not only talking about overnight vacations in five-star hotels, either. Any trip, even a daytime drive to another town, involves a certain level of relational commitment. People don't just jump into the car with someone they've never met before. Unless they're being kidnapped. Or haven't grown out of their love-beads-and-hitchhiking phase.

Traveling companions share a bond of some sort. Intentionally being with someone else on a journey presumes a connection. At the very least, an interest in the same destination. That's probably why I feel awkward when smashed up against a strange businessman on a petite plane. You really should have experienced dinner and a movie before having to sit inches apart and intertwine elbows for two hours.

Obviously, Solomon and Shulamith's relation-ship has matured to a whole new level when he invites her to take a trip with him:

> *My beloved speaks and says to me:*
> *"Arise, my love, my beautiful one, and come away,*
> *for behold, the winter is past;*
> *the rain is over and gone.*
> *The flowers appear on the earth,*
> *the time of singing has come,*

and the voice of the turtledove
is heard in our land.
The fig tree ripens its figs,
and the vines are in blossom;
they give forth fragrance.
Arise, my love, my beautiful one, and come away."

Song of Solomon 2:10-13

It's also significant that he invites her on a *spring* excursion. A season when tulips bloom tall and bright, baby birds chirp food orders to hovering parents, and daffodils dot the ground with explosions of yellow and white. It's a time when *everything* seems to be breaking free from the chilly confines of winter. Not only is it a great time to get out of the house and go for a romantic stroll—like Solomon and his fiancée—it's a time of celebration for *all* of God's beloved.

Watchman Nee, a wonderful Chinese theologian and devotional writer, teaches that the rain in verse 11 symbolizes the bone-chilling precipitation January and February are noted for.[3] The kind of wet, yucky weather that makes you want to huddle inside by the fireplace under a quilt with a cup of hot chocolate.

Mr. Nee goes on to explain that these verses illuminate our position as the redeemed bride of Christ. Because when spring is mentioned *after* winter in biblical poetry, it illustrates the miracle of resurrection that followed our Savior's crucifixion.[4] Thus, *scriptural springtime* represents the new life available to us as a result of the Cross. We can walk out of the frigid darkness into a glorious new season—blooming, if you will—because Jesus took the worst of winter with Him on Calvary.

Read Psalm 23, which describes a stroll that David took with the Lord. What's your favorite "green pasture" place, somewhere you go to be alone with God?

Fox-Proof Fencing

When I moved to a cottage in the country almost a year ago, visions of idyllic quaintness danced in my head. Now that I'd be twenty miles removed from the hustle and bustle of Nashville, I imagined a more peaceful existence. I planned to spend quality time drinking sweet tea on the wraparound porch. I planned to ponder deep things in the swing. I planned to take long walks in the woods. And the very pinnacle of my daydreams involved a large garden, full of heirloom tomatoes and raspberries and basil and such.

So a few months ago, I started taking steps to realize the garden. I called my little brother, John Price, who drives a truck and worked for a tobacco

did you know?

The fig tree was arguably the second-most important tree in ancient Israel, after the olive tree. It was a symbol of peace and security (see 1 Kings 4:22-25 and Zechariah 3:6-10). The fig tree blossoms in mid to late March, announcing the arrival of spring. The first figs that appear are sterile—basically "fake" figs that are not too tasty—followed by a second, edible fruit that ripens in August or September. Figs were also a common sexual symbol in the Ancient Near East.[5]

grower when he was in high school, making him practically a farming expert in my estimation. We chatted at length, strategizing when, where, and what to plant. After a while, we decided it'd be worth him flying up from Florida to help for a weekend.

Soon after J. P. arrived, we made our first trip to Home Depot. We rented a heavy duty rototiller to plow up the hard-packed Tennessee dirt. Several bone-jarring hours later, we returned the tiller and picked up the lumber needed for the garden fence. We also rented a pneumatic nail gun to speed up the process—and an auger—with more horse-power than small cars—to make postholes.

Finally, after two days of hard work and spending enough money to *buy* fresh produce for at least a decade, *Project Garden* was finished. Complete with a white, crosshatched fence, which would've been quaint, had my "manly man" baby brother not insisted on making it six feet tall! An old-timer drove up when we were making the final touches and expressed curiosity about the abnormally high barrier. I explained that it was to keep rabbits and deer out of my vegeta-bles. He sat in his truck considering this for a long minute, then said with a slow drawl, "That fence'll keep *giraffes* out of your vegetables."

The fence has been standing for three months now, guarding a cornucopia of berries, peppers, squash, and herbs. And while I may be the laugh-ingstock of every farmer who drives by my mini-Alcatraz, not one single varmint has plun-dered the garden. Plus, I've been savoring abso-lutely *delicious* tomatoes almost every day!

Solomon might have grinned and winked at my little brother's soaring barrier as well. Because after running over hill and dale to be with his date, gazing at her adoringly, and inviting her to join him on a spring stroll, he expresses the need to keep destructive varmints out of their relationship:

> *Catch the foxes for us,*
> *the little foxes*
> *that spoil the vineyards,*
> *for our vineyards are in blossom.*

Song of Solomon 2:15

Some scholars accuse this verse of being difficult to interpret. Evidently the Hebrew here is problematic, with possible double entendres and wordplay. They're not even sure that Solomon is the one calling for the fox hunt. It could actually be Shulamith who's expressing her fear of romance-ruining wolf wannabes. But what is crystal clear is the desire to protect their love from danger. To protect it from things that seem innocuous at first yet have the potential to destroy a relationship.

Things like jealousy. Impatience. Inconsideration. Even dubious huggers.

A friend of mine is married to a man who refuses to hug other women for *any* reason. Of course, I didn't know that when I was first getting to know them and found out the hard way one night after enjoying dinner at their house. I went to give him a quick side squeeze as I was thanking him for doing all the cooking. As I did so, he sidestepped my gesture, leaving me groping nothing but air.

I tottered a moment, feeling embarrassed and thinking maybe I'd eaten too much of the garlic bread.

But then I found out halitosis wasn't the issue. The reason he refuses even the most platonic physical affection from other women is that he's determined to honor his wife. His goal is to behave in such a way that she is completely secure in their relationship, that she never has any reason to worry about him wandering. And he's especially vigilant because her first marriage was sabotaged by adultery.

Some might think him overly cautious. I think he's a prince.

What "little fox" relationship saboteurs are you the most prone to (i.e. getting jealous, having a short temper, judging with a critical spirit, etc.)?

Even more important than protecting a human relationship is the necessity of guarding our relationship with God. We must be on the lookout for the seemingly small things that can infect the intimacy we have with Him. Things like busyness, gossip, and sleeping in on Sundays. Ask Christian friends to help keep you alert. Pray for a high, thorny hedge of spiritual protection. Guard your heart from the little foxes of unfaithfulness. Don't let the enemy get close enough to hug you. Even if it seems harmless.

DVD **Read Proverbs 4:23. How would you paraphrase this verse in your own words? What's the best way to build a figurative fence to protect your relationship with Jesus Christ?**

5

Lost and Found

You'd think that since I'm focused on some of the most romantic poetry ever written, I'd hit the blind date jackpot. That I'd be swept off my forty-something feet by a Solomonish guy before this book deadline comes and goes. But actually the opposite seems to be happening. My friend Julie (in the DVD) is now calling it my *"Perfect Storm* season of singleness!" I feel like a cookbook author who's infamous for setting kitchen fires. My romantic life has simply been abysmal. And I had the worst blind date *ever* this past weekend, which is saying a lot, since I've been set up with such a wide variety of men from grandpas to gropers.

A friend called a few weeks ago and invited me to her niece's wedding to meet Mr. Wonderful. I balked, because I thought it'd be weird to attend the union of two people I didn't know with the ulterior motive of meeting a potential boyfriend. But she begged, saying, "I promise it won't be weird! And you *have* to come because he's really excited about meeting you!" She went on to explain that some mutual friends would be there so I'd have someone to sit with and talk to.

I was still feeling apprehensive when I walked under a candlelit canopy of trees into the backyard where the wedding was being held. It didn't help matters that the new shoes I'd bought (which I hoped would enhance my legs) to go with the new outfit (which I hoped would disguise my middle) were sinking in the dirt like garden stakes with each step. In order to keep from making a trail of divots, I attempted to walk up the grassy hill gracefully while balancing on the soles of the new shoes. Which of course made me feel like a klutz instead of a great catch for some unattached man.

But I must say the wedding was beautiful. I got teary watching the radiant, young bride walk down the path of rose petals—even though I'd never met her before. And when my friend rushed over to point out the man I was supposed to meet, I was pleased that he looked to be about my age. As fate would have it, I ended up standing directly behind him in the reception line.

Then I happened to glance down and notice that he was holding hands with the woman beside him. And it didn't look like she was some grandmother

that he was gallantly escorting either. Here I was, standing approximately six inches behind the man I was supposed to be introduced to, and he was with a *date*! Ugh. I should've stayed home with a good movie and a Lean Cuisine. I considered making a run for it in my dagger-heels. Better yet, I thought about using the shoes to poke little holes in my matchmaking pal!

While it's kind of an amusing anecdote now, it wasn't very funny when it happened. I felt foolish and embarrassed. Being stood up in public was much worse than not having a date at all. It was like getting a pie in the face when I was expecting to shake hands. I had hoped to meet a nice guy, perhaps strike up a conversation. Maybe go out for coffee later. Instead I got a big serving of humiliation. The desire for intimacy can open up a Pandora's box of pain.

Read Song of Songs chapter 3 in the New Living Translation or *The Message* and synopsize this chapter in your own words.

Read Proverbs 20:5-9 and Romans 7:22-25. Do you think human love relationships can ever be completely painless? Why or why not?

Maybe you've never had a blind date debacle like mine, but I'll bet you've experienced the exquisite sadness that offsets joy. Or the loneliness that's often the flipside of romance, the grief that replaces giddiness when love slips through your fingers.

That's the situation Shulamith finds herself in at the beginning of chapter 3:

On my bed by night
I sought him whom my soul loves;
I sought him, but found him not.

Song of Solomon 3:1

Some Bible commentators think she's just having a bad dream here. Others think she's awake, but tossing and turning, afraid their love affair won't last. Either way there's a desperate poignancy in her words. You can almost hear the catch in her throat and the urgency in her pitch when she says, *I'm looking for the man I'm in love with, but I can't find him. I'm all alone again.*

Moving Mountains

Not too long ago, CNN and all the major television networks were buzzing with news about an eleven-year-old little boy, Brennan Hawkins, who got lost in the wilderness near a Boy Scout camp in Utah. There was moving footage of his anguished parents, who hoped for his safe return, and coverage of the search and rescue teams who were combing the mountains to find him. Then finally, heartwarming images of Brennan being found were broadcast around the world.

Marney Rich Keenan, a reporter with *The Detroit News*, described the situation like this:

> *During the recent four days when the mountains were being combed for any sign of Brennan Hawkins, news outlets posted his fifth-grade class picture it seemed almost endlessly. Typical elemen-*

MORE INFO

The words *by night* in verse 1 are plural in the original Hebrew poetry. Therefore, this phrasing could be clearer if it read, *night after night*, indicating they've been separated for a while, not simply one night.[1]

*tary school photo: fake smile, hair without benefit of
a comb. You'd look at it and think: What a cute
kid, hope they find him. . . .*

*Surely, everyone was amazed, if not tearful,
watching Brennan Hawkins being unloaded from
the ambulance, so sunburned his lips were swollen,
his ears beet-red, but in such good condition, all he
needed was his parents' arms wrapped around him
from now until forever.[2]*

The person many others (including Ms. Keenan)
single out as the real hero in young Brennan's
recovery is a man named Kevin Bardsley. Although
he's a private citizen, not a member of the official
law enforcement team, he played a key role. He
helped organize volunteers. He paid for much of
the necessary equipment: maps, heavy-duty lights,
two-way radios, and more.

Essentially, Kevin Bardsley "captained" the
search for Brennan. He knew how to keep things
moving forward. How to coordinate helicopters and
tracking dogs and people on horseback. How to
keep tired volunteers motivated. Mr. Bardsley was
knowledgeable and passionate about finding
Brennan because his little boy, a twelve-year-old
named Garrett, had gone missing in the exact same
area the previous summer. And his son hasn't been
found yet.

**Have you ever *momentarily* lost someone you
love—like a child in a department store? If so,
describe how you felt while they were missing.**

Much like Kevin Bardsley, when Shulamith discovers that Solomon is missing, she leaps into action:

> *I will rise now and go about the city,*
> *in the streets and in the squares;*
> *I will seek him whom my soul loves.*
> *I sought him, but found him not.*
> *The watchmen found me*
> *as they went about in the city.*
> *"Have you seen him whom my soul loves?"*
>
> Song of Solomon 3:2-3

What lengths would you go to if your spouse, or child, or friend, or family member turned up missing? My guess is that you'd go to great lengths to find them. You'd have the police on speed dial. You'd pester the FBI to get involved. You'd put up flyers and call radio stations and organize prayer vigils. You wouldn't care about sleep or food or how much the search cost. You'd stand at the foot of the proverbial mountain and shove with all your might for as long as it took.

It's a shame we don't respond with the same vigor when our passion for God goes missing. When our security in Christ is kidnapped. When our desire for His Word disappears.

Following a torrid extramarital affair, during which he had his mistress Bathsheba's unsuspecting husband killed, King David lost the intimacy he had with God. A friend of his, Nathan, was the first to suggest a search party, which became a rescue effort that David threw himself into with all of his contrite heart:

Purge me with hyssop, and I shall be clean;
wash me, and I shall be whiter than snow.
Let me hear joy and gladness;
let the bones that you have broken rejoice.
Hide your face from my sins,
and blot out all my iniquities.
Create in me a clean heart, O God,
and renew a right spirit within me.
Cast me not away from your presence,
and take not your Holy Spirit from me.
Restore to me the joy of your salvation,
and uphold me with a willing spirit.

Psalm 51:7-12

King David yearned to recover the closeness with Abba—*Daddy*—that he'd lost through sin. He knew what it felt like to be in God's presence. To walk and talk with Him. To receive counsel and wisdom and protection and provision from the Alpha and Omega. A life without that divine intimacy wasn't an option for him.

MORE INFO

Bathsheba—the woman David had an affair with and then married after instigating her husband Uriah's homicide—was also Solomon's mother. Solomon was actually their *second* son; their first son (who was conceived while Bathsheba was still married to Uriah) died as a consequence of David's sin. For the unabridged account of this tumultuous true story, read 2 Samuel 11-12.

Which adjectives best describe your relationship with God right now: *vibrant and growing, holding steady, waning, stagnant,* **or** *nonexistent?* **If your relationship falls into the latter categories, what steps are you taking to find missing intimacy with God?**

Eureka, I Found Him!

One of the reasons that Brennan's story was front-page fodder, that CBS's *The Early Show* interviewed his exultant family, and that *People* included it in their celebrity-gossip oriented rag is because it ended happily. Against the sorrowful backdrop of the thousands of other missing children who are never returned to anxious mommies and daddies, Brennan came back home. He was found.

Solomon was too:

> *Scarcely had I passed them*
> *when I found him whom my soul loves.*
> *I held him, and would not let him go*
> *until I had brought him into my mother's house,*
> *and into the chamber of her who conceived me.*
>
> Song of Solomon 3:4

My youngest nephew, John Michael, adores my aunt Darlene. I think he'd rather go to her house than to Toys "R" Us! They have a blast singing in the car, splashing in the pool, and teasing each other. He's been enamored with her animated personality since he was a baby. As a matter of fact, among his first phrases was the sweetly possessive "*my* Darlene."

One of my favorite lines in this entire poem is when Shulamith says, *I held him, and would not let him go.* She finally has her beloved back and nobody's going to pry her fingers off. She's stuck to him like Velcro! Author and Song of Songs expert, Dr. Craig Glickman puts it this way: "Her heartfelt desire for Solomon is at a pinnacle of intensity. When choosing a marriage partner, it's sound

advice to select not just someone you can live with but someone you cannot live without. Shulamith has found that person."[3]

What relationships do you hang on to the tightest? Who will you *not let go* of?

Pop culture seems preoccupied with "healthy" relationships (although there doesn't appear to be a consensus regarding what *healthy* actually means). Television personalities and radio hosts and books encourage us to embrace our independence, to resist being defined by someone else, to avoid emotional ownership. I'll admit, that does sound pretty healthy! Unless you're applying that pseudopsychology to God, the Lover of our souls.

Remember, the lens through which we're looking at this biblical poetry is *Christological.* That means Shulamith loosely represents us. And she's pictured here in chapter 3 with a white-knuckled grip on Solomon. She's not celebrating her singleness or trying to suppress feelings of possessiveness; she's *clinging* to her man! The kind of posture a repentant King David describes regarding God:

> *My soul clings to you; your right hand upholds me.*
>   Psalm 63:8

There is no better relationship than the one we can have with God, available to us through faith in Jesus Christ. No one will ever love us like He does. No one can be as compassionate. And no one can understand us like God does because He created us.

NOTES

He is the *best thing* that will ever happen to us. So go ahead, be clingy!

> *But whatever gain I had, I counted as loss for the sake of Christ. Indeed, I count everything as loss because of the surpassing worth of knowing Christ Jesus my Lord.* Philippians 3:7–8

Read Song of Songs 3:5. This is the second time Shulamith asks her friends to help hold her accountable with regards to sexual purity with Solomon. Why do you think she repeats the request?

Everyone Loves a Parade

Cindy Welchel, my best friend in high school, had an older sister named Linda whom we thought was the epitome of coolness and beauty. She looked a lot like Princess Diana and carried herself with that same regal grace. But she didn't *act* like a stereotypical princess. She was never condescending to those of us who looked up to her. We probably acted like pests half the time, but she always put up with us. I don't remember her ever saying an unkind word to me.

So it was fitting that the best-looking guy in church fell for her. His name was Jeff; he was tall and blond and broad shouldered. Kind of Brad Pitt meets Robert Redford, with a little bit of Billy Graham thrown in. All of us high school girls would practically faint when he glanced in our direction. We all had huge, unrequited crushes on Jeff! But since we knew we were really too young for him, we were thrilled when he asked out our heroine, Linda Welchel.

Their courtship seemed like a Hollywood romance unfolding in front of us. We hung on every word she said about him. I think we were as excited as Linda was when Jeff asked her to marry him! And the wedding definitely seemed like something out of a movie. She was so beautiful in her white dress, and he looked every bit the handsome prince. Then, after reciting their vows, they walked outside and climbed into a horse-drawn carriage and rolled away, just like Charles and Di—although Jeff and Linda are still married all these years later, I might add.

Aside from your own—if you're married—what's the most beautiful wedding ceremony you've ever attended? What made it memorable?

There's something special about the pageantry surrounding the wedding of two people who are madly in love with each other. And when Solomon and Shulamith's royal ceremony finally rolls around, the pomp and circumstance is spectacular!

> *What is that coming up from the wilderness*
> *like columns of smoke,*
> *perfumed with myrrh and frankincense,*
> *with all the fragrant powders of a merchant?*
> *Behold, it is the litter of Solomon!*
> *Around it are sixty mighty men,*
> *some of the mighty men of Israel,*
> *all of them wearing swords*
> *and expert in war,*
> *each with his sword at his thigh,*

against terror by night.
King Solomon made himself a carriage
from the wood of Lebanon.
He made its posts of silver,
its back of gold, its seat of purple;
its interior was inlaid with love
by the daughters of Jerusalem.

Song of Solomon 3:6-10

The imagery of smoke columns in the wilderness was very familiar to the Jewish wedding guests. What Old Testament symbolism does it remind you of? Read Exodus 13:17-22 if you need to jog your memory.

Prince Charming looks like a pauper compared to this guy! Solomon is coming up the hill outside Jerusalem in a *carriage*. Which probably means that he's actually being carried on a fancy "people-platter" (think of the ornate bed the princess was ferried around on in *Aladdin*, not the pumpkin cab Cinderella took home), on the shoulders of his soldiers. His is a mode of transportation fit for a real king, a royal monarch who is considered to be one of the wealthiest men in history. Solomon's twenty-four karat carriage wasn't anything like the tour bus I rode in when I visited Jerusalem!

Can you imagine what Shulamith is thinking? Remember, it hasn't been that long since she was working her fanny off in the family vineyard. And she still has calluses on her hands from the Weed Eater to prove it. She wasn't sure then that she'd ever get married. Now here she is, watching the

king of Israel coming toward her on a big purple pillow with silver posts. She can't believe how blessed she is . . . it's like she's been zapped into a living fairytale!

Read Psalm 45. There are some interesting similarities between Song of Songs 3:6-10 and this psalm, which is also a love song. Yet both have definite military overtones. Would you describe anything about the military—or soldiers in general—as *romantic*?

When I was a sophomore in college, my friend Carmal set me up with her boyfriend's best friend, Joe. The four of us went to a skating rink on "Christian College Night," and somewhere between rolling around in fast circles as Petra blared through the speakers and then slowing down during the Sandi Patty songs, Joe and I fell in like. By the time an Amy Grant tune was chosen for the "couple's skate" serenade, we were holding hands. And by the time the weekend was over, Joe and I were smitten with each other.

Therefore, we were both disappointed that before we met he'd already made plans for a long trip to another state. The night before he left he gave me one of his old football jerseys to sleep in and asked for one of my old T-shirts in return. Neither one of us was looking forward to the separation, so we said good-bye with sad faces. I was describing the details of his departure to Carmal the next morning, when we noticed someone running across the campus. The person was racing

NOTES

up a hill and seemed to be headed our way.

We stopped walking and started staring, riveted by the runner's enthusiasm and by what looked to be a cape, flapping wildly over his head. He looked like some kind of miniature Superman, without the tights. But when he got closer, I recognized the "cape" as my well-worn T-shirt. And I was tickled to see Joe's red face—grinning from ear to ear—underneath it!

He breathlessly explained that he had postponed the trip by a day and was coming to whisk me away for lunch and an afternoon at the beach. I was a little flustered by his fervor, but also glad that Carmal witnessed it. Because he was just so adorable!

I picture Shulamith watching Solomon's arrival with wide eyes and one hand covering the smile on her face. She's probably a little embarrassed by his grand gesture, but she also thinks he's darling. Especially with the little *flower hat* his mom, Bathsheba, made him wear! So she tells her girlfriends to check him out:

> **MORE INFO**
>
> The Hebrew word for *crown* in verse 11 doesn't mean a coronation crown, which would have to be administered by a high priest or divine representative, but a symbol of joy and celebration, like the laurel wreaths given out at the early Olympic games.[4]

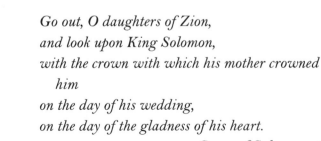

> *Go out, O daughters of Zion,*
> *and look upon King Solomon,*
> *with the crown with which his mother crowned*
> *   him*
> *on the day of his wedding,*
> *on the day of the gladness of his heart.*
>
> Song of Solomon 3:11

As extravagant as this parade was, it will pale next to the royal wedding between the Prince of Peace and His bride, the church. Solomon's arrival will be nothing compared to our Savior splitting the clouds to claim us for all eternity. I can't even imagine what we'll be thinking when Jesus appears, riding toward us on a white horse, wearing a luminescent robe embroidered with the words, *King of kings and Lord of lords.*

> *Then I saw a new heaven and a new earth, for the first heaven and the first earth had passed away, and the sea was no more. And I saw the holy city, new Jerusalem, coming down out of heaven from God, prepared as the bride adorned for her husband. And I heard a loud voice from the throne saying, "Behold, the dwelling place of God is with man. He will dwell with them, and they will be his people, and God himself will be with them as their God. He will wipe away every tear from their eyes, and death shall be no more, neither shall there be mourning nor crying nor pain anymore, for the former things have passed away."*
>
> Revelation 21:1-4

If you got to design a literal wedding dress to meet Jesus in, what would it look like?

6

Too Hot to Trot

How do I love thee? Let me count the ways.
I love thee to the depth and breadth and height
My soul can reach, when feeling out of sight
For the ends of Being and ideal Grace.
I love thee to the level of everyday's
Most quiet need, by sun and candle-light.
I love thee freely, as men strive for Right;
I love thee purely, as they turn from Praise.
I love thee with the passion put to use
In my old griefs, and with my childhood's faith.
I love thee with a love I seemed to lose
With my lost saints, I love thee with the breath,
Smiles, tears, of all my life! and, if God choose,
I shall but love thee better after death.

Elizabeth Barrett Browning, "Sonnet XLIII"

Benjamin, the son of my best friend Kim (who's in
the On the Road DVDs), has been begging for a
pet for as long as I can remember. His requests

began with desperate pleas for a puppy, which Kim tried hard to resist.

But Benji finally broke through Kim's *no-pets-in-my-house* stance when he told her tearfully that he'd be happy with just one teensy, little hamster. Of course, this moving confession took place after he'd been home sick for a few weeks, so her defenses were down. Within an hour or so after returning home from the pet superstore—after having spent over a hundred dollars on pet paraphernalia—Benji announced that he didn't want the hamster after all. Evidently, the little rat had bitten him several times, and he was certain they'd picked out a defective animal.

Now I absolutely adore Kim's boys but let me tell you, if I were a domestic rodent and Benji were my master, I'd take a chunk out of an appendage too, mainly to discourage him from using me as a football or dance partner. Kim was understandably exasperated. Here she had wilted under the I'm-the-only-petless-child-in-America assault, and now her son wanted to take it back! So she impatiently informed him that the hamster bit him because he wouldn't stop pestering it. She told him to leave the poor thing alone and allow it to settle down. Benji hung his head in disappointment, still convinced the hamster they had purchased was a *lemon*.

Both mother and son were surprised when they woke up a few mornings later to find eleven baby furballs. Their hamster hadn't been defective, she had been pregnant! No wonder she was so grouchy—all she wanted to do was eat pickles and

ice cream and take a nap in fresh sawdust. But
instead she had been sold to a boy who treated her
like a Frisbee!

Things are not always what they appear to be.
Especially when it comes to biblical poetry. Which
brings us to the "sex" chapter in Solomon's Song!

**Read Song of Songs chapter 4 in the New Living
Translation or *The Message* and synopsize this
chapter in your own words.**

Reread Psalm 139:13-14. Without qualification,
**what would you say is your best physical
feature?**

A Barnyard Body

Unlike Ms. Browning's lovely poetry, these Old
Testament metaphors don't come across as very
romantic at first:

> *Behold, you are beautiful, my love,*
> *behold, you are beautiful!*
> *Your eyes are doves*
> *behind your veil.*
> *Your hair is like a flock of goats*
> *leaping down the slopes of Gilead.*
> *Your teeth are like a flock of shorn ewes*
> *that have come up from the washing,*
> *all of which bear twins,*
> *and not one among them has lost its young.*
> *Your lips are like a scarlet thread,*
> *and your mouth is lovely.*
> *Your cheeks are like halves of a pomegranate*
> *behind your veil.*

Your neck is like the tower of David,
built in rows of stone;
on it hang a thousand shields,
all of them shields of warriors.
Your two breasts are like two fawns,
twins of a gazelle,
that graze among the lilies.

Song of Solomon 4:1–5

Hmmm. I can kind of understand the dove comment. And the whole scarlet thread–mouth comparison. However, I might be less than flattered if some guy told me my hair reminded him of goats, my teeth looked like sheep, and my neck resembled a stone tower. I think I would excuse

did you know?

In the early 1900s, British archaeologists discovered a scroll—now titled **Papyrus Harris 500** and preserved in the British Museum in London—from the burial tomb of the Egyptian Pharaoh, **Ramses II** (1290–1224 BC). This scroll contained nineteen erotic Egyptian love songs, and though it appears to have been written almost a thousand years before Solomon's era, they are very similar in style. For instance, one lyric, ascribed to the man, says,

My lover is a marsh,
My lover is lush with growth . . .
Her mouth is a lotus bud,
Her breasts are mandrake blossoms,
Her arms are vines,
Her eyes are shaded like berries.
Her head is a trap built from branches . . .
And I am the goose.
Her hair is bait in the trap . . .
To ensnare me.[1]

myself, race to the bathroom, and whip out a comb
and a toothbrush. Not to mention, change into a
turtleneck sweater!

Although the words Solomon uses to describe
Shulamith's beauty wouldn't be effective pickup
lines in our culture, they were actually extremely
flattering in his day. We just need to understand
the ancient Israeli symbolism.

Mount Gilead is a prominent area in
Jewish history (see Genesis 31:20-23;
Deuteronomy 3:13, 16; Deuteronomy
34:1-4; Judges 20:1; and 2 Samuel
17:24-26), and most likely, a prominent
place in Solomon's *personal* history. He
probably had great memories of camp-
ing there with his dad, King David. He
had probably sat by their tent and
watched goatherds descend the nearby
peak. Like the horses I admire galloping
across green canvases near my house,
I bet those black goats cascading down Mount
Gilead made the entire hillside come to life!

> **MORE INFO**
>
> Chapter 4 introduces the
> image of a veil—*Your eyes are
> doves behind your veil*—which
> underscores the marriage
> aspect in this section of the
> poem. Normally, Hebrew
> women wore headdresses, but
> not *veils*, except for special
> occasions like engagement
> parties and wedding celebra-
> tions (See Genesis 24:65;
> 29:23-25).[2]

Thus, when Solomon compares Shulamith's hair
to goats, he's not implying that she needs to wash
it. Or that she should switch salons. He's rhapso-
dizing about how gorgeous her long, wavy
tresses are.

With similar nostalgia, he compares her teeth to
ewes with crew cuts. Like his father before him,
Solomon probably had a summer job on a sheep
farm when he was a teenager. Surely he remem-
bered how bright they looked after being helped
out of their wool coats, how the baby lambs were

identical bleating bundles. Therefore, he doesn't mean her teeth are fuzzy when he associates them with sheep; he's saying they're perfectly matched and very white. She doesn't need braces or bleaching or pricey veneers. Her smile is already dazzling.

Another seemingly left-handed observation draws our attention from Shulamith's head to her neck: *Your neck is like the tower of David, built in rows of stone.* But he's not hinting for her to cut back on her workouts. He's not trying to tell her that she's developing the physique of a football player from lifting so many barrels in the vineyard. He's saying she has an elegant neck, one he'd like to cover with kisses. And by linking it to *the tower of David* and *shields of warriors,* he's giving her the ultimate in masculine approval, kind of like when a man compares a woman's figure to a Ferrari. Brimming with testosterone, Solomon uses military metaphors to praise Shulamith's strength of character.

Then we come to the part of the poem that has the power to make adults shift nervously in church. The infamous verse that becomes an elephant in coed Sunday school classrooms. And Solomon doesn't take it easy on us here, either. He doesn't use a Christian code word or bland euphemism; he just comes right out and says, *breasts.* Then, before bashful Bible readers have time to recover, he throws us further off balance by comparing them to gazelle babies:

> *Your breasts are like fawns, twins of a gazelle, grazing among the first spring flowers.*
>
> Song of Songs 4:5 (*The Message*)

Solomon's wild animal simile may not be as easily grasped as a romance paperback's tacky *heaving-bosom-in-a-torn-bodice* description, but it is much more lyrically imaginative. By comparing Shulamith's décolletage to young deer, he's telling her that her breasts look so soft and sweet he'd really like to pet them!

What's the most flattering thing anyone's ever said about your body?

Besotted with Beloved

I think it takes a very strong man to admit that he's head over heels in love with a woman, much less to wax poetic about her. He risks being maligned by his buddies, being excommunicated from secret male-bonding societies, and being typecast as a wimp. Only the bravest Romeos can survive this Darwinian love gauntlet. But those who do, win the hearts of women everywhere. And the grudging respect of their male friends.

Menelaus, the King of Greece, was that kind of man. According to the blind poet Homer, a prince called Alexander (also known as *Paris* or *Prince of Troy*) fell hard for Mrs. Menelaus, the queen. Her name was Helen. Supposedly, Alexander was so infatuated with Helen that he snuck into the palace and kidnapped her. When Menelaus discovered his bride was missing, he drafted the entire Greek army to get her back. The memory of her beautiful face inspired him to launch a thousand ships.

Sam Baldwin—the widowed architect and

FAST FACT
Pomegranates were a common source of food and decorative symbolism in the Ancient Near East. Furthermore, pomegranate wine was considered to be an aphrodisiac in Egypt, and was used in "love potions."[3]

father portrayed by actor Tom Hanks in the movie, *Sleepless in Seattle*—was also that kind of man. When asked by the intrusive radio talk-show host, Dr. Marsha, what made his late wife so special, Sam/Tom replies, "It was a million tiny things, that when you add up meant we were supposed to be together. And I knew it. I knew it the very first time I touched her. It was like coming home—only to no home I'd ever known. I was just taking her hand to help her out of a car . . . and I knew it." While he's reminiscing, he wears this heart-wrenchingly wistful expression. And Jonah, his precocious movie son, is asleep in his lap. You just *know*—along with Annie Reed/Meg Ryan—that Sam was completely in love with his wife.

Was your dad an affectionate man when you were growing up? Do you wish he'd been *more* or *less* demonstrative about his love for you?

Certainly Solomon, who either wrote or inspired this song of all songs, is that kind of man. He's declared his affection for Shulamith in private and in public. On spring picnics and in lavish parades. He's been a bold Romeo, a courageous suitor. His desire for her has been unmistakable. And his pièce de résistance, his personal poetic best, the culmination of this amazing epistle of love, occurs in the middle of chapter 4:

> *You have captivated my heart,*
> *my sister, my bride;*
> *you have captivated my heart*

with one glance of your eyes,
with one jewel of your necklace.

Song of Solomon 4:9

Solomon ignores the tittering of adolescent wedding guests. He doesn't care that the royal caterer forgot the canapés for the reception. He doesn't even notice the raised eyebrows of his buddies, fidgeting nearby in their rented tuxedos. He only has eyes for his gorgeous bride. She has completely captured his heart.

If you're married, describe what you felt like when you said your vows. Did you repeat the traditional phrase, *Till death do us part?*

Shulamith Responds

I knew a girl in high school who was friends with almost everyone, but a girlfriend to no one. She had a great sense of humor and was well liked, but guys just didn't seem interested in dating her. One day, when we were driving to the mall together, she asked me what sex was like with my long-term boyfriend. I was surprised by the question, but I also detected notes of genuine sadness and confusion in her voice. So I explained that he and I didn't have a sexual relationship, that because we were committed to Christ, we were committed to sexual purity until marriage. I told her it was sometimes a difficult struggle, but we believed sex was worth waiting for. Then I asked her why she brought the issue up. And though the conversation took place over twenty years ago, I can still remember her response.

She told me how one of her closest male friends

FAST FACT

When the term **brother** or **sister** is used in biblical poetry, it is an expression of endearment, common in Ancient Near East literature. The phrasing **does not** imply an incestuous relationship; it refers to closeness and permanence.

had come to her house drunk a few weeks before. He had asked her to go for a ride with him. Then he parked by the lakefront and asked her to get in the backseat with him. She lost her virginity when they had quick, unprotected, unromantic sex. She told me that he mumbled that she might want to use a feminine hygiene product when he dropped her off so she wouldn't get pregnant. Since that first encounter, this boy had come by late at night for "favors" several times. And then she cried. She couldn't understand why he was being such a jerk to her at school now that she'd given him her body.

I felt so sorry for her. She had been duped by a guy who would take her virginity but wouldn't take her to a football game. I knew it wasn't supposed to be like that. I knew that you weren't supposed to feel dirty and used and humiliated after being physically intimate with someone.

 Aside from semantics, how would you describe the major emotional differences between *having sex* and *making love*?

The bride and bridegroom at the wedding I recently attended (the blind-date-calamity night) made a striking pair. They were young and tall and blond. She looked like a model and he resembled a professional tennis player. Since they'd been dating for three years, they had that familiar, affectionate, connected posture when they stood next to each other. It was also common knowledge they were passionate Christians and both virgins.

When the ceremony was over and the pastor

pronounced them man and wife, I overheard
several people make teasing comments about the
fact that they probably wouldn't stay at the reception very long. Rumor had it that the bridegroom
told the bride she had a whopping ten minutes
before he was whisking her away to their honeymoon suite! And from the way she gazed at him
throughout the nuptials, I don't think she cared
one bit about cutting the cake.

Solomon's ongoing narrative regarding
Shulamith makes it clear that she was a
virgin too:

> *A garden locked is my sister, my bride,*
> *a spring locked, a fountain sealed.*
>
> Song of Solomon 4:12

Here she is, standing before her adoring groom
in the palace bedroom. Her wedding dress is piled
on a chair in the corner. Through the window she
can hear noises from the wedding party continuing
outside. She's never been alone with a man like this
before. No other man has been given the right to
gaze at her naked body. To other men she was a
locked garden and sealed fountain. This is her first
sexual encounter. But while she's inexperienced,
she certainly doesn't appear nervous or restrained.
As a matter of fact, her reaction to his erotic invitation is an enthusiastic "Yes!"

> *Awake, O north wind,*
> *and come, O south wind!*
> *Blow upon my garden,*
> *let its spices flow.*

NOTES

Let my beloved come to his garden,
and eat its choicest fruits.

Song of Solomon 4:16

Shulamith looks forward to making love with Solomon because she is secure in their relationship. He had been open with his affection, along with his intention to marry her. Furthermore, he had been willing to wait for sex. He recognized that her virginity was a treasure, not to be opened until he made a lifetime covenant with her. Unlike my friend's horrible high school experience, this portrayal of sexual intercourse is not crass or demeaning. It's a wholly appropriate, passionate expression of commitment and intimacy.

In most Christian circles, marriage is considered to be a sacrament. How would you define *sacrament* in your own words?

7

A Thundering Ovation

LIFE LIVED INSIDE THE CONTOURS OF GOD'S LAW
HUMANIZES US AND MAKES US BEAUTIFUL.

Lauren Winner, Real Sex

Several years ago I was invited to teach at a Christian singles' conference. I must confess that I don't normally attend such gatherings willingly. In such settings I've met too many women who subscribe to *Bride* magazine without a date on the horizon and too many middle-aged men who still live with their mothers. The organizers of this particular event wanted me to lead a seminar on "Singles and Sexuality." One would assume that they didn't need to pay someone to fly across the country to hold a discourse on this subject. It seems like anyone could have said, "If you're single, you can't have sex," and that would've been the end of it. I'm not sure why the baton was passed to me. But for some reason, I agreed to speak.

What's more, as if to confirm my negative suspicions about singles' events, the conference started out with an embarrassing bang. Right before I stepped up to the podium, a married pastor glanced at me with kind pity and then blurted into the microphone, "Lisa is a beautiful, successful, *celibate* single woman!" I was so flustered by his qualification that I didn't know quite how to respond. It was nice of him to exaggerate about my looks and imply that I'd accomplished something, but I felt like a deer (not a baby deer, mind you) in the headlights when the word *celibate* reverberated through the sound system.

That emcee's public announcement about my hibernating libido is just one example of how the subject of sex can make people uncomfortable. Especially when many of us harbor different ideas of what it's supposed to be like in the first place.

- Women who were marginalized in backseats when they were younger are prone to view sex as degrading. Or they might see sex as an opportunistic tool with which to manipulate others.
- Men who've perverted their views about sex through pornography often associate it with lust, power, and subjugation. (Dennis Rader, the notorious "BTK Strangler" who was recently captured and convicted of torturing and killing at least ten people in Kansas, said his gruesome murder spree was an expression of sexual fantasy.)

- Baby Boomers and Gen Xers guzzling a steady stream of movies, cable television, and popular fiction are likely to rationalize that sex is a trendy accessory or sign of success. That the more frequent and varied your experience, the greater your hip factor.
- Modern adolescents are mass programmed by MTV and pop culture to think of sex as a rite of passage. Like climbing a mountain, sexual promiscuity brings with it certain bragging rights.
- And those who consider themselves to be committed evangelicals are inclined to think that sexuality is a "dirty deed."

Read Song of Songs chapter 5 in the New Living Translation or *The Message* and synopsize this chapter in your own words.

Would you describe most of the people in your social circles as "casual" or "chaste" when it comes to the topic of sex? How would you describe yourself?

Is Paul Sexually Paranoid?

We don't have the time—and I don't have the expertise—to debunk all of the contemporary "sex myths" that permeate subgroups in our society. But we can examine the one right under our nose.
I firmly believe that Christians often have a warped outlook on sexuality because of our scriptural illiteracy. Most of us simply don't understand what God has to say about it. And those who have

Exegesis
critical explanation or interpretation of a text or portion of a text, especially of the Bible.[1]

memorized verses that encompass marriage or physical intimacy tend to misunderstand them.

For instance, if you're reading this book in a church small group or Bible study environment, you've probably already had at least one person bring up Paul's words in 1 Corinthians:

> *Now concerning the matters about which you wrote: "It is good for a man not to have sexual relations with a woman." But because of the temptation to sexual immorality, each man should have his own wife and each woman her own husband. The husband should give to his wife her conjugal rights, and likewise the wife to her husband.*
>
> 1 Corinthians 7:1-3

If that person is squirming right now, the wriggle is justified. It's dangerous to pick a few verses out of the Bible to prove a point. Or to create your own "holier-than-thou" doctrine without a thorough exegetical understanding of the subject at hand. Paul was *not* teaching something contrary to the "Sex is Beautiful" anthem in Solomon's Song. He wasn't implying that it had become a scab on the knee of humanity. And he certainly wasn't declaring some kind of holy war against physical intimacy in marriage.

The apostle Paul was writing to first-century Christians who lived in a wildly promiscuous culture, where homosexuality, prostitution, and even bestiality were commonplace. So he was emphasizing the fact that

MORE INFO

Porneia is a Greek word that's used over fifty times in the New Testament. It's translated alternatively as fornication, lust, and sexual immorality. It's one of the main words Paul uses when warning Christians what kind of behavior to avoid. Additionally, *porne*—etymologically related to *porneia*—is the Greek word for prostitute. Both *porne* and *porneia* are roots of the English word *pornography*.[2]

marriage is God's sole provision for sexual fulfill-
ment. This missionary, whom many Bible scholars
think was widowed, also makes the practical point
that it's easier to focus on Christ when you *aren't*
dealing with the emotional responsibilities of
marriage than when you *are.*

**Read Ephesians 5:25-33. How does this passage
effectively refute Paul's reputation as an
"antimarriage" writer?**

Although Paul's advice is moot in my present
marital condition, his words did come to mind
recently while I was having lunch with an old
friend. After a few minutes of small talk, she
lowered her voice to confess something that had
happened the week before. She and her husband are
followers of Christ, but there'd been a bit of trouble
in their corner of paradise.

She said she was upstairs on the landing and he
was sitting in a recliner on the first floor. She called
an important question to him and when he didn't
answer, she looked down to find him engrossed in a
football game on TV. She was so fed up with his
habit of ignoring her while reading the paper or
watching sports that she intentionally dropped the
heavy dictionary she was carrying over the railing
to get his attention. She didn't mean for it to land
squarely on his head!

My married friends tell me an incident like that is
just a small blip on the radar of a till-death-do-
us-part relationship. They say every marriage is
bound to have seasons of ecstasy and agony. Our

pastor, Scotty Smith, calls it the "rupture and rapture" of marriage. He says the person you fell head over heels in love with also has the ability to frustrate, exasperate, and irritate you like no one else; that your spouse's most endearing qualities can morph into the most annoying.

That insight, along with Paul's counsel to the Corinthian believers, helps me remember to count my single blessings when I'm feeling particularly whiny about not being married. I'll bet it *is* easier to focus on a Bible study when you don't have to listen to football on television. I'm sure it *is* easier to peruse Old Testament poetry when you're not expected to cook someone else's dinner.

Read Galatians 5:16-26. Although *fruit* is singular in this passage—meaning you possess the whole list if you're a Christian—which of these godly traits is not as "ripe" as the rest in your life? What scenario can provoke you to bypass the fruit list altogether and throw heavy things like anger or sarcasm at your spouse, children, friends, or family?

A Vigorous God-Nod

I'm sure some of you are anxious to move past all this ultra personal stuff and get to the next section in the Song of Songs. You've been patient, but like the dictionary-dropper, you've had about all you can take. You're probably thinking, *If I wanted to concentrate on sex, I could just watch a soap opera or pick up a book with a damsel in distress and a pirate on the cover.* Please hang in there though, because

we're almost finished with our tour of sex city!
Almost. But first we need to make one final stop.

When I was in high school, I worked part-time
in a ladies' clothing store called The Vogue. Let me
clarify that this store didn't have anything to do
with Madonna and her silly song about "vogueing,"
nor did we sell tacky undergarments like that
pointy metal bra she wore in the music video. The
Vogue I worked in only carried refined, high-end
women's apparel, sold by a classy sales staff—with
the exception of me. I got the job because my mom
bought a lot of clothes there!

Due to my inexperience and the fact that we
were on commission, one of the older employees—
whom we'll call Grumpy—didn't like me very
much. When we worked the night shift together,
she told me I had to clean the restroom and take
out the trash because she had bunions and needed
to sit down. When she made mistakes on the cash
register, she blamed it on me. She was masterful at
swooping in and stealing my sales; evidently her
feet felt fine then. And she had a way of saying
hateful things in a nice way.

Once, when I returned home from college for a
holiday break and was asked to help out at the
store, Grumpy met me at the door with everyone
else. She stood back while we all hugged and
exchanged greetings. Then, when the reunion
quieted down but everyone was still gathered
around, she exclaimed with a perky smile, "My
goodness, Lisa! You sure look like you've gained *a
lot* of weight!" I could feel my face turning red, even
though I'd actually lost weight that semester and

was pretty thin. Grumpy was so good at feigning friendliness while lobbing mean-spirited grenades. Her heart and her voice were in sharp contrast. Her tone was pleasant but her intentions were not.

Some people assume God is like Grumpy when it comes to sex. They think that while His Word allows sex if you're married, Jehovah actually prefers prudishness. Even though it's technically permitted, sex is really more like a mulligan in golf: You only make use of it if you absolutely have to.

Lauren Winner, author of *Girl Meets God*, says this about how believers distort the issue of sexuality in her recent offering, *Real Sex*:

> Cosmo *and* Maxim *aren't the only places that lie. The Christian community—the church—also perpetuates some false ideas about sex. The church's intention, no doubt, is noble and laudable, but in its fervent determination to preserve sex for marriage in a broader culture that is ever more hostile to Christian sexual ethics, the church tells a few fibs of its own.*[3]

She spells out the top three Christian sex fibs like this: Premarital sex is guaranteed to make you feel lousy; women don't really want to have sex, anyway; and bodies (and sex) are gross, dirty, or just plain unimportant.[4]

Which of the above sexual "fibs" have you heard implied most often in Christian settings? Why do you think these statements are able to masquerade as *godly conclusions*?

I certainly haven't spent the time researching modern sexuality the way Lauren Winner has, but I think her observations are right on target. Most of the Christians I know seem to be looking at sex through smudged lenses. I've watched married women in church grimace when the subject is broached. I'm pretty sure they don't think God is cheering them on with pom-poms when they're dancing between the sheets.

Yet that image is very close to what God says after Solomon and Shulamith consummate their marriage:

> *Eat, friends, drink,*
> *and be drunk with love!*   Song of Solomon 5:1

Most Bible scholars and seminarians agree that these words come directly from God's mouth. That He is the "unseen but present guest in their bedroom."[5] He has observed every kiss, every caress, every intimate detail of their lovemaking, and His response is essentially, "Go for it!" One commentator explains God's reaction like this:

> *He lifts His voice and gives hearty approval to the entire night. He vigorously endorses and affirms the love of this couple. He takes pleasure in what has taken place. He is glad they have drunk deeply of the fountain of love. Two of His own have experienced love in all the beauty and fervor and purity that He intended for them. In fact, He urges them on to more. . . . That is His attitude toward the giving of their love to each other. And by the way, that's also His attitude toward couples today.[6]*

An Autobiographical Explanation

Celebrate with me, friends! Raise your glasses—
"To life! To love!"

Song of Songs 5:1 (*The Message*)

So why does a single chick like me care about a sexy scriptural place like this? Well, I can assure you it's not because I'm a masochistic voyeur. I'm merely a Bible student who thinks God's original portrait of physical intimacy has been vandalized by sin. And I think the potential for delight in human sexuality is an effective backdrop for the *superlative* message of the delight available to us in Christ.

If you'll remember King David's words—*Because your steadfast love is better than life, my lips will praise you* (Psalm 63:3)—you can see that every possible experience here on earth pales next to the intimacy we can have with our heavenly Father. Now think about how spectacular that first night of passion was for Solomon and Shulamith, or how spectacu-lar sex can be in *any* Christian marriage, (I'm not naive enough to think that it's *always* spectacular because we live in a fallen world full of dirty dishes, stressful jobs, and hormone imbalances, but I'm sure every couple has a "personal best.") Isn't it awesome to realize that God's love for us is *even brighter* than those physical and emotional fireworks?

The bottom line is that at its very best, human sexuality is wonderful . . . but God's love is way better! Plus, God won't roll away from us in the middle of the night. Or say He has a headache. Or

ignore us during the Super Bowl. Or have to get in the mood before He embraces us. God's love for *all* of us—whether you're a hot married mama or a blind-date disaster waiting to happen—is consistently, perfectly amazing.

> *This inebriation makes people sober. This inebriation is one of grace, not of intoxication. It leads to joy, not to befuddlement. In the banquet hall of the church there will be pleasant odors, delightful food and drink in variety. There will be noble guests and attendants who grace that occasion. It will not be otherwise! What is there that is nobler than to have Christ at the church's banquet, as one who ministers and is ministered unto?*[7]

> Ambrose of Milan
> AD 333–397, commenting on Song of Songs 5:1

8

When Delight Turns to Drudgery

OUR CALLING IS NOT JUST TO BE THE FAITHFUL BRIDE, BUT
ALSO THE BRIDE-IN-LOVE. A BRIDE HAS NOT BEEN FAITHFUL
JUST BECAUSE SHE HAS NOT SLEPT WITH ANYONE ELSE.

Francis Schaeffer

Recently I sat near a little boy who was experiencing his very first plane flight. He was in the window seat, peering out the porthole, narrating everything to his mom, who was sitting between us. He enthusiastically described the size and shape of every piece of luggage that was crawling up the conveyer belt into the belly of our aircraft. Then squealing with excitement when another jet pulled up to the gate next to ours, the little boy shifted his attention to that plane's particulars. His voice increased in speed and volume during our taxi and takeoff. But once we were in the air, he was curiously silent.

I glanced over his mother's magazine to make sure he hadn't swallowed a peanut or something and was graced by the sight of a six-year-old in awe. His eyes were wide and his mouth formed a silent *O*. When he recovered his voice and resumed his commentary, I closed my book, leaned back against the headrest, and really listened. It was delightful to hear him compare the clouds to cotton candy and the houses below us to ants.

After seeing his cherubic face illuminated with wonder, I realized I was a jaded frequent flyer. Riding in winged metal tubes is something I do to get from one city to another. I hardly even notice the scenery anymore. What was considered an outlandish impossibility before Orville and Wilber Wright's inaugural journey a little more than a hundred years ago—and nothing short of a miracle immediately afterward—has become a mundane chore to me.

Read Song of Songs chapter 6 in the New Living Translation or *The Message* and synopsize this chapter in your own words.

In spite of the conjugal pyrotechnics of their honeymoon, the act of loving soon became a chore for Shulamith, too:

> *I slept, but my heart was awake.*
> *A sound! My beloved is knocking.*

"Open to me, my sister, my love,
my dove, my perfect one,
for my head is wet with dew,
my locks with the drops of the night."
I had put off my garment;
how could I put it on?
I had bathed my feet;
how could I soil them?

Song of Solomon 5:2-3

She's snug as a bug under the brocade duvet they received as a wedding gift, when Solomon comes home late from a business dinner. She woke up when the garage door opened, but she's so comfortable in her cocoon that she pretends to still be asleep when he tiptoes into the room. When he sits down softly on the bed and starts rubbing her back, she holds her breath and hopes he'll go away. Maybe he'll fix himself a bowl of ice cream or

did you know?

Some commentators—all **much** more erudite than I—teach that the beginning of chapter 5 in the Song of Songs (5:2-8) is either a dream sequence or some kind of fictional motif.[1] However, at least two notable Bible scholars insist that's not the only option. G. Lloyd Carr (a respected seminary professor and pastor with advanced degrees in theology, including a PhD) praised Craig Glickman's (a lauded academic, professor, and author with two doctorates) "more realistic" approach in his volume concerning the Song: "This section, particularly vv. 2 and 3, records the tender approach of the lover and the unexpected apathy and indifference of the beloved to his overtures. It was a temporary lapse in their relationship, (v. 6), but certainly a common one between husband and wife, and, if continued, bears the seeds of the disintegration of the relationship."[2]

watch a game on TV. Instead he whispers, "Are you awake, baby?" She exhales with exasperation and says, "I am now."

Then when her new husband sweetly suggests some late night bonding, she blows him off by saying, "Ugh! I don't feel like getting all hot and bothered right now. I'm too tired and I don't want to take another shower. Can't you just leave me alone tonight?" Or something like that. Which is quite the juxtaposition to her previous "Come and blow on my garden, big boy" invitation!

Glickman offers this observation about Shulamith's change of heart:

> *The lengthy account of this next experience is rather surprising. After all, the Song isn't very long, so Solomon must be selective, highlighting the most significant aspects of their ideal romance. He has thus far described what one might expect: the birth of love; time alone in nature; awakening of sexual desire; patience in waiting; anxiety when apart; wedding day and night.*
>
> *I would have guessed the next important snapshot would be of their new home or the birth of a child. Instead, the Song recounts the problem of the princess taking Solomon for granted. The songwriter knows that apathy will wither this love that had begun in thankful tears. So he shows us the critical need for appreciation to make love grow.*[4]

MORE INFO

The exact Hebrew phase translated "how could I" in Song of Solomon 5:3, occurs only one other time in the Bible, in the story of Esther. When Esther throws herself at the mercy of her new husband, King Ahasuerus, in order to save the Jews from Haman's evil extermination plan, she says, "For how can I bear to see the calamity that is coming to my people? Or how can I bear to see the destruction of my kindred?" (Esther 8:6)[3]

Did Shulamith's "boredom in the bedroom" surprise you, or did you see it coming?

The Danger of Spiritual Lethargy

Shulamith's petulance in the bedroom points to the biblical truism that intimacy grows in an environment of humility and gratitude—with others and with God. Indifference and apathy will kill a relationship just as sure as Roundup kills weeds. Perhaps that's why Jesus saved His harshest rebuke for a motley crew of lazy believers:

> *I know your works: you are neither cold nor hot.*
> *Would that you were either cold or hot! So, because*
> *you are lukewarm, and neither hot nor cold, I will*
> *spit you out of my mouth.*   Revelation 3:15-16

Those severe words were literally directed at a first-century church plant in a place called Laodicea. Archaeologists tell us this city was known for its banks, textile industry, and the manufacture of a unique eye ointment,[5] which was a big seller in drugstores throughout Asia Minor.

Squinting tourists flocked to Laodicea to pay homage to the lime-rich spring water, which was the active ingredient in this early version of Visine. They paid a dollar for a map and a trolley ride to the river, then hopped off expecting to see a beautiful, flowing stream. What they found instead was a tepid, slow-moving trickle, choked with green slime.

But the people living there didn't care that their water source was gross, because they got rich off it. The "miracle drops" paid for their fancy homes and foreign cars and giant plasma screen televisions. And their preoccupation with materialism led to a loss of spiritual passion: *I mean, really, who cares about going to hear some guy talk about "taking up your cross daily" or "washing other people's nasty feet" when you can stay home in your pajamas and watch a movie with surround sound?* Or so they thought.

I wonder if they were jolted from their spiritual stupor when they got John's dog-eared letter, with the none-too-subtle lukewarm reference, accusing them of rolling their eyes at God. I wonder what kind of buzz went through their well-dressed crowd when they heard that their laxity made Jesus gag. I wonder if the hotshot bankers and factory owners and CEOs were embarrassed when they read how the Messiah characterized them as *wretched, pitiable, poor, blind, and naked* (Revelation 3:17). More important, I wonder if they accepted His unwarranted offer of forgiveness:

> *Those whom I love, I reprove and discipline, so be zealous and repent.* Revelation 3:19

Apathy is a dangerous disease that hardens spiritual arteries and causes heart failure. The most effective prescription for it is a dose of repentance, swallowed with humility. And gratitude has been found to be very effective in preventing it.

Read 1 Timothy 6:10. Why do you think Paul associates loving money with evil? Do you think there's a connection between materialism and spiritual passivity? If so, explain why.

Spiritual Sweat Equity

You probably remember that Shulamith realized
that Solomon was missing once before, just prior to
their wedding in chapter 3 (vv. 1-4). And that
episode wrapped up quickly when she found him
and vowed to never let him go. But this time his
departure is different. It's not just happenstance or
a harmless misunderstanding, like he ran out to get
a midnight snack at Taco Bell and forgot to take
his cell phone. This time it was her fault. Her
bedroom rebuff made him disappear like a magi-
cian's rabbit.

When she realizes the unfortunate effect of her
behavior, Shulamith takes off after Solomon wearing nothing but a negligee:

> *I opened to my beloved,*
> *but my beloved had turned and gone.*
> *My soul failed me when he spoke.*
> *I sought him, but found him not;*
> *I called him, but he gave no answer.*
> *The watchmen found me*
> *as they went about in the city;*
> *they beat me, they bruised me,*
> *they took away my veil,*
> *those watchmen of the walls.*
> *I adjure you, O daughters of Jerusalem,*
> *if you find my beloved,*
> *that you tell him*
> *I am sick with love.*

Song of Solomon 5:6-8

Due to the symbolism of this divine poetry—
"sexy" sheep and grooms leaping over mountains

like a Diana Ross lyric—Bible scholars aren't definitive about whether the abusive guards in this passage are literal or metaphorical. Although, if a young girl was found running around half-dressed in the middle of the night during the time this book was written, the punishment described here was customary.[6] Courtney Love's habit of wearing a nightgown in public would have definitely been frowned on in the Ancient Near East.

But whether she was literally beaten or just beaten down emotionally, Shulamith's second search for Solomon proves to be difficult. She doesn't find him right away. She suffers severe relational consequences as a result of her selfishness. And she has to work hard to bridge the gap that she initiated.

Share about a time when you had a disagreement with a spouse or friend which resulted in a rift. How did you reconcile with that person? Do you think compromise is a *good thing* or a *cop-out* in close relationships? Explain.

In the last chapter, we attempted to dismantle a few distorted ideas about sexual intimacy. Now we need to take apart the assumption that emotional intimacy with God will be a constant reality, or an ever-increasing commodity, like Microsoft before the tech market stumbled. We must eradicate the foolish notion that "deep" Christians—which is an ambiguous term at best, and arrogant if you think you are one—won't ever suffer the consequences of spiritual apathy.

Frankly, I don't always *feel* like loving God. Sometimes I act just like Shulamith did with Solomon; I roll over and feign sleep when the Holy Spirit whispers. I can relate to Paul's admission in Romans:

> *For I know that nothing good dwells in me, that is, in my flesh. For I have the desire to do what is right, but not the ability to carry it out. For I do not do the good I want, but the evil I do not want is what I keep on doing.*
>
> Romans 7:18-19

It's silly to assume that once you confess faith in Christ, you'll naturally wake up every morning humming a worship song, that you'll gain immediate profundity every time you search the Scriptures, that you'll be transported to a place of scented candles, warm fuzzies, and serenity every time you shoot up a quick "drive-thru" prayer, that you'll always feel connected to His holy hip.

MORE INFO

1 Thessalonians 5:16-18 paints a more admirable picture of the apostle Paul—when his attitude is being governed by the Holy Spirit. Remember, he wrote these words after being stoned, beaten with metal rods, and thrown into prison (Acts 14, 16)!

Intimacy with God is not something to be taken for granted. There will inevitably be seasons of separation, just like Shulamith and Paul demonstrate, because of our sin. Our petulant flesh is prone to build walls that separate us from the nearness God gladly and generously allows.

Take some time to read Ephesians 2 slowly. What light does this passage shed on the issue of feeling far away from God?

It behooves us to remember the awe we first had about God's unconditional love. How we were wide-eyed and openmouthed with wonder, like that little boy on the plane. How thankful we were that He called us "sweetheart." How God's grace prompted us to scoot as close as we could through long conversational prayers, marinating in His Word, and spending quality time in worship with other people who love Him. And in those seasons that we discover the closeness we once had in Christ missing, we must *search for it*—no matter how difficult the recovery process.

DVD Read James 1:22-25. Although a relationship with God is available only by His grace and not any "work" on our part (Ephesians 2:8-9), what does this passage imply about the responsibility we do have regarding nearness to God?

The Art of Appreciation

Once a month I teach a Bible study at the Hope Center, a faith-based residential program for women that's run by the Nashville Union Rescue Mission. The women there are all working through difficult issues. Some were sexually abused when they were little girls. Some were burned with cigarettes. Some have spent time in prison. Most have struggled with drug and alcohol abuse. Most have suffered the indignity of homelessness at one time or another. And yet they are the most radiant, honest group of people I've ever had the privilege of spending time with.

Recently, I got to visit with one of the residents,

a big, bright, beautiful, brown woman with an infectious grin. I asked her how she ended up at the Hope Center, and she responded with two words, "crack cocaine." Then she described how she first smoked crack with the man who fathered her only child. He was arrested for possession on the day she was in the hospital giving birth to their son. And even though that man was soon killed— largely because of his drug habit—how she *still* became enamored with those deadly narcotic rocks he introduced her to.

She forfeited the better part of fifteen years to a cycle of getting high, breaking the hearts of those who loved her, then promising them she'd quit. Until one morning, after disappearing on a three-day bender to celebrate her birthday, she opened the door of the home she shared with her now-teenaged son and mother to find the house empty. She frantically called them to find out what happened and her son answered his cell phone. He sadly informed her, "We've moved, Momma. And Granny says I can't tell you where we are."

She said that's when she realized she had to get serious help, when she counted the casualties of her personal battle with drugs. Recognizing the value of what she stood to lose is what finally compelled her to get real about rehab.

Toward the end of this dramatic search for Solomon, Shulamith also recognizes the value of the relationship she stands to lose. And much like the conversations that take place in the hallways of the Hope Center, she describes her realization to some girlfriends, the daughters of Jerusalem:

My beloved is radiant and ruddy,
distinguished among ten thousand.
His head is the finest gold;
his locks are wavy,
black as a raven.
His eyes are like doves
beside streams of water;
bathed in milk,
sitting beside a full pool.
His cheeks are like beds of spices,
mounds of sweet-smelling herbs.
His lips are lilies,
dripping liquid myrrh.
His arms are rods of gold,
set with jewels.
His body is polished ivory,
bedecked with sapphires.
His legs are alabaster columns,
set on bases of gold.
His appearance is like Lebanon,
choice as the cedars.
His mouth is most sweet,
and he is altogether desirable.
This is my beloved and this is my friend,
O daughters of Jerusalem.

Song of Solomon 5:10-16

This is the only extended section, or *poem within a poem*, of the Song where Shulamith extols the virtues of her husband, and boy, is it a doozy! She starts by praising his outdoorsy complexion and goes on to compliment his wavy black hair, masculine arms, and good-looking legs. She also enthuses about other body parts, but we won't go there out of deference to demure readers (for the not-so-prim, check out the note about ivory).

And my favorite part of her appreciative oration is when she says, *This is my beloved and this is my friend.* Because it reminds me of the words Jesus declared about *us* in the Gospel of John:

> *No longer do I call you servants, for the servant does not know what his master is doing; but I have called you friends, for all that I have heard from my Father I have made known to you.*

John 15:15

Although we can be just as apathetic and selfish as Shulamith was, the Lord Jesus mercifully calls us His friends. What a miracle!

My mother often encouraged me to "count my blessings"; in fact that hymn was one of her favorites when I was growing up. In what way do you think *Count your blessings, name them one by one* helps relationships stay on track?

MORE INFO

I'll bet most commentators blushed when dissecting the Hebrew text in verse 14, because the word *ivory* brings to mind a "tusk" and many think it's an erotic phallic symbol,[7] which certainly compliments the eroticism of the garden motif in 4:12-13.

9

Recovering the Romance

KEEP YOUR FEET DRY, YOUR EYES OPEN, YOUR HEART AT
PEACE, AND YOUR SOUL IN THE JOY OF CHRIST.

Thomas Merton

A few weeks ago, I had coffee at Starbucks with my
friend Ann. She was still glowing from time on the
beach at St. Barts where she and her husband,
Allen, had recently celebrated their twenty-fifth
anniversary. And she was really animated about
what happened on their vacation. They shared
moonlit walks and candlelit dinners and passionate
alone time. It was the ultimate in romantic
getaways!

But their marriage wasn't always romantic like
that. As a matter of fact, the first half of their rela-

tionship was more of a blur than a newlywed season of emotional bonding. They met at an ultraconservative Christian college, where makeup, jewelry, and even wedding rings were forbidden, and married a few years later in a ceremony that Ann laughingly refers to as, "With this *watch*, I thee wed."

Then Allen went to medical school, which was followed by seven years of surgical residency. During this time Ann gave birth to three babies in quick succession. She also became an expert at packing and unpacking boxes because they moved six times in order to accommodate Allen's medical career before finally settling in Nashville.

Allen is the first to admit that while he loved Ann, he didn't show it very much during the first fifteen or so years together. He'd been raised in a rigid, undemonstrative home where touching and saying things like "I love you" and "I'm sorry" were rare occurrences. His parents applauded his performance, yet ignored his heart. So he developed into a brilliant, driven surgeon, who typically bumbled the emotional intricacies of relationship. He was successful at the hospital, but not so adept in the home.

Ann says the lack of tenderness that characterized the initial season of their marriage is what made her so desperate for Christ. And Allen now says it was her love affair with Jesus that taught him how to express affection. He says that her increasing devotion to God, which resulted in selfless love toward him and the kids, is what finally melted his cold heart. He confessed this to Ann in a

letter he gave her in St. Barts—just before handing her a small velvet box that held a big diamond ring.

They both gave me permission to print these excerpts:

May 4, 2005

My only love,
Most elementary school students are able to pen a simple list of affections for their chosen. As you have longingly recognized, I rarely do and when asked, often poorly.

Did I miss the line for nurturing? Was I out to lunch when patience and longsuffering were passed out? Maybe I was operating when contentment was being awarded. Yet I find my desire for these things real. This desire arises from my wish to offer to you that which is so often given. . . .

Almost every day in the midst of true chaos, some-times in the elevator or driving in traffic, I long for you. I'm never certain what sparks this desire, when I'm so justifiably preoccupied. Occasionally, I will see a couple walking, their manner conveying easy love and familiarity. A look will pass between them— silent, well-understood language—that seems imme-diately ours. A girl will touch a guy and I know that touch.

The providence of God seems most clear when reviewing my life, and there you are. What I did not even know I needed was provided. This unending, tolerant, forgiving love. The love that desires me when I do not desire even myself. This permissive, secure love. Your love that endures my mood, demeanor. This love relaxes, enjoys, and shares. It runs through our home and the lives of our precious children. It brings me to its source like a bee to honey.

As we marvel at our years, the answer to, "How did you do it? What's the secret?" has never been more clear. It remains what I treasure most: your love. It excites me, comforts me, heals me. It binds us, protects us, nurtures our injuries, strengthens our resolve, motivates and prompts me to love in a like manner.

As we spend these days together, I find contentment. As I reflect on years together, pleasure and completeness. I am excited by these days, no less than the anticipation of the days and years ahead. I resolve to love in the way I've been loved. I resolve to pursue and allow pursuit. I am resolved to love, dare I say, "love you well," for I am loved well.

Besides proving that unlike old dogs, some husbands *can* learn new tricks, this letter reveals that gratitude fertilizes intimacy. When Allen recognized how precious the gift of love was that Ann had given freely, he moved toward her. When he finally learned to share his feelings, she found they were certainly worth waiting for.

(By the way, just in case you're looking for a sensitive heart surgeon, you won't find "Allen" in the phone book because their names have been changed to protect their privacy!)

Read Song of Songs chapter 7 in the New Living Translation or *The Message* and synopsize this chapter in your own words.

Read Psalm 92:1-4. How would you paraphrase these verses in the form of a short love note to God?

Much Better than Manure

Chapter 6 of the Song is woven with themes of gratitude. Shulamith is thankful that Solomon quickly forgives her cold-shoulder treatment, and he's grateful that she came looking for him. Both are thrilled that their first lover's quarrel didn't mean a lengthy stay at the Holiday Inn.

And his sigh of relief is followed by a stream of praise not unlike the words in Allen's love letter:

> *You are beautiful as Tirzah, my love,*
> *lovely as Jerusalem,*
> *awesome as an army with banners.*
> *Turn away your eyes from me,*
> *for they overwhelm me . . .*
> *My dove, my perfect one, is the only one,*
> *the only one of her mother,*
> *pure to her who bore her.*
> *The young women saw her and called*
> *   her blessed;*
> *the queens and concubines also,*
> *   and they praised her.*
>
> Song of Solomon 6:4-5, 9

MORE INFO

Song of Solomon 6:10: *Who is this who looks down like the dawn, beautiful as the moon, bright as the sun, awesome as an army of banners?* is most likely the exclamation of Shulamith's girlfriends—the daughters of Jerusalem—who'd been wringing their hands, anxiously awaiting the outcome of her first fight with Solomon. It declares their collective delight that all is well in this biblical Camelot once more![1]

If you're married, are your closest friends more likely to *affirm* that relationship or *sabotage* it? Do you ever initiate or welcome negative comments from others about your spouse when you're mad at him?

Solomon's thankfulness for Shulamith is clear in this sweet moment of reconciliation. He compares her to the most beautiful cities in Israel. Then he expounds by saying that out of all the women he's ever known, he's never met anyone quite like her. And his appreciation works like Miracle-Gro on their relationship.

Just look at how she responds to his love language:

> *I went down to the nut orchard*
> *to look at the blossoms of the valley,*
> *to see whether the vines had budded,*
> *whether the pomegranates were in bloom.*

Song of Solomon 6:11

Those who reddened over the ivory tusk reference in the last chapter might want to leave the room if you're perusing this with friends, or turn the page if you're reading this in solitude. Because with these words, our young bride is sending Solomon a boldly sensuous message. When she counters his complimentary description by telling him about her trip to the "nut orchard," she's not talking about pistachios. She's talking about the unbridled passion they had on their honeymoon!

One of my married girlfriends and I were chatting about this passage and she bobbed her head in enthusiastic agreement with Shulamith's behavior. She said, "When my husband sincerely appreciates me verbally, it's *very* effective

MORE INFO

The Hebrew word for "orchard" is *ginnat*, and is closely related to the Hebrew word *gannâ*, which is translated *garden* in the Song. Thus, the word *orchard* is an explicit reference to the sexual intimacy they'd experienced. Furthermore, the word *nut* was probably a slang term for male genitalia, just as it is in our culture.[2]

foreplay!" And while I don't have any personal examples regarding a nuptial response, I've found that other relationships respond very favorably to some well-placed "thank-yous," too. Albeit, minus the endorphins.

Read Psalm 100. Since few of us will ever enter a church literally shouting, "Thank you, God!" how can we practically *enter his gates with thanksgiving?*

Unsatisfactory Substitutes

As I write this I'm sitting in my favorite spot, in one of my favorite coffee shops. A bright, comfy place in Franklin, Tennessee, called Kozibean. It's sort of like the bar Cheers, but instead of Ted Danson serving me a beer, Shannon or Crockett Bone, who own this place and always remember my name, serve me java. However, today I'm not drinking my favorite liquid dessert: a rich, fattening combination of dark chocolate, 2 percent milk, espresso, and whipped cream. I'm not drinking that concoction because my clothes are getting too tight, and because I've had enough caffeine in the last few weeks to choke one of those Budweiser horses. Thus, I'm drinking lukewarm tea with soy. And let me tell you, it's definitely not hitting the spot!

In light of the explicit sexual overtones in this Biblical poetry, it's important to note that lust is a *terrible* substitute for love. When Solomon brags

> **MORE INFO**
>
> The word *tôdāh* (pronounced toe-dah), is the Hebrew word for "thanksgiving." It's used about thirty times in the Old Testament, such as in the Psalms when gratitude is being expressed (Psalm 26:6-7, ESV; 42:4, *The Message*). And it's preserved in the modern Hebrew language as the every-day word for "thanks."[3] So if you lived in a Jewish community today and someone said, "Your haircut sure is cute," you'd respond with a cheerful, "*tôdāh!*"

about Shulamith, he is gentle and tender. He doesn't speak in crude terms or act like a boorish brute with nothing but sex on his mind. He even asks her to look away: *Turn away your eyes from me, for they overwhelm me.* While he's very attracted to her, he doesn't want to risk injuring her heart by jumping immediately into bed after their falling out.

Read Ephesians 5:22-33. Now describe the Biblical legitimacy of the phrase, "selfless lover."

I know a woman who was married to a stinker who quoted another verse from Ephesians: "Be angry and do not sin; do not let the sun go down on your anger" (Ephesians 4:26) whenever they had an argument. Then he'd bully her with the warning that she'd better have sex with him right then or else she'd be "in sin." When she cried and begged him not to make her, he still demanded to have his way. He manipulated God's Word to satisfy his own lust. And in so doing, he sowed damaging seeds in their marriage, which ultimately ended in divorce.

Solomon isn't like that. In spite of his wealth and power he doesn't treat Shulamith like someone who exists primarily to quench his sexual appetite, like a stick of gum that he could chew and then spit out the window after it lost its flavor. He cherishes his wife. He values her companionship.

And based on the faith the Bible says Solomon had in God (1 Kings 3), he knows better than to expect his spouse to meet all of his needs—even if she is the most amazing individual he's ever met.

Do you think it's possible to love another person "too much"? How can you tell the difference between *committed love between two humans* and *idolatry* or *lust*?

In their groundbreaking book, *Bold Love*, Drs. Dan Allender and Tremper Longman teach that physical lust—which is both a desire for union and the desire to be "absorbed" into another person[4]— is a poor substitute for *worship*:

> *Our hearts desperately long for Eden. We want fullness of self that removes the stark, brittle light of self-consciousness. Our hearts, in other words, live for an experience of worship that fills our beings with a joy that is so deeply in awe of the other that we are barely aware of ourselves. Sexual immorality, or adulterous lust, provides a tragic counterfeit of a loss of self that also enhances the self. It inevitably leads to even more empty, self-consuming despair.[5]*

How did a distorted view of worship lead to the first murder recorded in biblical history? If you aren't sure, read Genesis 4:1-11.

Another significant book by Edward Welch, called *Addictions: A Banquet in the Grave* stresses that all additions—sex, alcohol, food, drugs, relationships, etc.—are ultimately *a disorder of worship*.[6] In other words, when we attempt to satiate ourselves with people, emotions, experiences, or artificial substances, we're trying to plug up a vacuum that only God can fill.

NOTES

The Rolling Stones Were Right

In May 1965, Mick Jagger brought his now-famous lips close to a studio microphone and sang the grammatically challenged lyrics of a song that he and bandmate Keith Richards had written just a few days earlier. And while it was a "hooky" tune, they debated whether or not to include it on the record they were making because they thought it might sound too much like the song "Dancing in the Street" by Martha and the Vandellas. Ultimately they decided to include it.[7]

A month later, "Satisfaction" roared up the charts to become the Rolling Stones' first number one hit in the United States. It was a familiar anthem during the antiestablishment 1960s and '70s, and now, forty years later, it still has the power to make balding dads and soccer moms close their eyes and play air guitar. Even if you were a church kid like me, you know the chorus:

> *I can't get no satisfaction*
> *I can't get no satisfaction*
> *'Cause I try and I try and I try and I try*

did you know?

Blaise Pascal, a brilliant seventeenth-century mathematician, philosopher, and physicist, has been credited with envisioning all kinds of amazing inventions—from calculators to trains—long before they actually became a reality. As imaginative as Pascal was, he knew that all the man-made things in the world cannot satisfy the human heart. That thought was expressed in what is probably Pascal's most famous quote: "There is a God shaped vacuum in the heart of every man which cannot be filled by any created thing, but only by God, the Creator, made known through Jesus."

I can't get no, I can't get no
No satisfaction

I wonder if the Rolling Stones knew they were
synopsizing the soteriology that Jesus explained to
the woman at the well:

> *A woman, a Samaritan, came to draw water.*
> *Jesus said, "Would you give me a drink of water?"*
> *(His disciples had gone to the village to buy food*
> *for lunch.)*
>
> *The Samaritan woman, taken aback, asked,*
> *"How come you, a Jew, are asking me, a Samari-*
> *tan woman, for a drink?" (Jews in those days*
> *wouldn't be caught dead talking to Samaritans.)*
>
> *Jesus answered, "If you knew the generosity of*
> *God and who I am, you would be asking me for a*
> *drink, and I would give you fresh, living water."*
>
> *The woman said, "Sir, you don't even have a*
> *bucket to draw with, and this well is deep. So how*
> *are you going to get this 'living water'? Are you a*
> *better man than our ancestor Jacob, who dug this*
> *well and drank from it, he and his sons and live-*
> *stock, and passed it down to us?"*
>
> *Jesus said, "Everyone who drinks this water*
> *will get thirsty again and again. Anyone who*
> *drinks the water I give will never thirst —not*
> *ever. The water I give will be an artesian spring*
> *within, gushing fountains of endless life."*
>
> *The woman said, "Sir, give me this water so*
> *I won't ever get thirsty, won't ever have to come*
> *back to this well again!"*
>
> John 4:7-15 (*The Message*)

You remember her, don't you? She was like the ancient version of Elizabeth Taylor; she'd been married and divorced five times and was now living with a man. Probably someone she'd met in a bar when he asked her to dance to a Rolling Stones' tune (well, I guess they aren't quite *that* old!) And she was flabbergasted when Jesus recounted her shabby romantic history, including her current live-in beau, before she revealed any personal information. She said something like, "How could you possibly know all that stuff about me? Are you some kind of a prophet or something?"

The Messiah answered her stupefied question by explaining God's plan of redemption. He told this outcast of a woman that she needed to be in a relationship with Him instead of all those goobers who just wanted to sleep with her. That she wouldn't get *any satisfaction* until she learned to worship Him.

Soteriology
the doctrine of salvation through Jesus Christ[8]

And the Greek word Jesus uses for "worship"— *proskuneō* —in their conversation by the water cooler is very significant. Especially when you consider all the proverbial toads that this girl has puckered up to. The roots of this worship-word are *pros*, meaning "toward," and *kuneō* which means "to kiss."[9] Jesus is basically saying, "Sweetheart, you've got to move toward Me with affection. Because I'm the only One who can give you the love you're longing for."

Humanly speaking, who gets the lion's share of your kisses?

As we near the end of this historic and poetic love story between Solomon and Shulamith, we need to focus on the bigger picture. We have to remember that this Polaroid of one couple's affection is eclipsed by the perfect biblical picture of a relationship with Jesus Christ. He is infinitely better than the most amazing human husband. Plus, you don't have to fret if you've never frolicked in the surf of St. Barts or gotten frisky in a pistachio grove, because we'll be honeymooning forever with Him in paradise!

Have you ever taken a vacation specifically to be alone with God? Like a spiritual honeymoon, a special rendezvous with your Redeemer? If so, what was it like? If not, perhaps you should plan one.

10

Marks of Maturity

WHETHER THE DAY IS STORMY OR FAIR, WHETHER I AM
SICK OR HEALTHY, WHETHER I FEEL LIKE A DIRT BALL OR
A BUTTERFLY, WHATEVER COMES CANNOT ALTER THE FACT
THAT THE LORD IS RISEN.
Brennan Manning, Reflections for Ragamuffins

Two months ago, my prayer-walking-pal, Lori, and
I visited our other talking-to-God-on-foot friend,
Emily, in the hospital. I brought a gift from
Pottery Barn Kids wrapped with a blue ribbon,
which was upstaged by Lori-the-knitting-phenom's
handmade blanket. We were shamelessly compet-
ing for baby Taylor's affection even though he was
less than twenty-four hours old!

I still can't believe Emily's a mom, much less the

mother of two children (Taylor's big sister is a darling and, dare-I-say, brilliant two-year-old named Anna.) It seems like only yesterday that Emily was a bright-eyed freshman in the high school girl's Bible study I was teaching. Frankly, she doesn't *look* much older than she did then. Or seem any worse for the wear. She still has the same blonde hair, lithe figure, and the joie de vivre that prompted her to roll down a hill and into a row of trees when she fell in love with Jason.

But she *is* different. She's been married to her beloved Jason for almost ten years now. She's delighted with and devoted to little Anna and Taylor. And she's even more passionate about Jesus than she was when we became friends fifteen years ago. Emily is all grown up.

Read Song of Songs chapter 8 in the New Living Translation or *The Message* and synopsize this chapter in your own words.

We've seen Shulamith mature in the course of the Song, as well. We met when she was a teenager, working full-time in vineyard management, and flush-in-young-love with Solomon. We grinned when she enthusiastically text-messaged replies to his flirtatious voice mails. We cheered alongside her girlfriends, the daughters of Jerusalem, when she walked down the aisle toward him—while he watched bug-eyed on that eggplant-colored pillow with his blossom hat all crooked! We furrowed our eyebrows and shook our heads sadly when she acted like a fanny early in their

marriage. We sighed with relief when she admitted her mistakes and they made up.

I apologize ahead of time for quoting a Britney Spears song title, but Shulamith is now past the "I'm Not A Girl, Not Yet A Woman" phase of her life. She's all grown up. And her husband, King Solomon, is well aware of her womanly attributes:

> *How beautiful and pleasant you are,*
> *O loved one, with all your delights!*
> *Your stature is like a palm tree,*
> *and your breasts are like its clusters.*
> *I say I will climb the palm tree*
> *and lay hold of its fruit.*
> *Oh may your breasts be like*
> *clusters of the vine,*
> *and the scent of your breath like apples,*
> *and your mouth like the best wine.*
>
> Song of Solomon 7:6-9

There's no need to explain much about this sensuous overture, because Solomon is pretty clear about Shulamith's body and his intentions! Although, his compliment about her breasts being like *clusters* is interesting. Especially when you remember how he described her chest in chapter 4:

> *Your two breasts are like two fawns,*
> *twins of a gazelle,*
> *that graze among the lilies.*
>
> Song of Solomon 4:5

MORE INFO

The Hebrew word for "palm tree" is *tāmār*, which is also the name of two notable women in the Bible—Judah's daughter-in-law (Genesis 38) and Amnon's half sister (2 Samuel 13). Both are involved in very sexually explicit dramas. This leads some commentators to suggest that the name *Tamar* could mean a sensual woman.[1]

It sounds like her top half used to be perky, but now it resembles *bunches* of dates or grapes, bringing to mind the adjective *hanging*. This would make sense because everyone breast-fed back then and there was no such thing as cosmetic surgery, so maintaining "perky" was pretty much impossible! More important, *clusters* of fruit implies that she is able to nourish. Her breasts used to be merely objects of beauty, pleasing to look at, soft to the touch. But with physical maturity, she can now feed children. She's gone from being a "still life" to actually providing food for life! Which—especially in light of the symbolism throughout this poem—makes me think she's probably matured in much the same way spiritually. She's probably grown into the type of godly woman that Paul talks about in Titus 2 (verses 3-5), one who nurtures others in their walk of faith.

DVD **Who depends on you for spiritual nourishment?**

Shulamith responds to Solomon's advances with more confidence than ever before:

> *Come, my beloved,*
> *let us go out into the fields*
> *and lodge in the villages;*
> *let us go out early to the vineyards*
> *and see whether the vines have budded,*
> *whether the grape blossoms have opened*
> *and the pomegranates are in bloom.*
> *There I will give you my love.*
> *The mandrakes give forth fragrance,*

and beside our doors are all choice fruits,
new as well as old,
which I have laid up for you,
    O my beloved.   Song of Solomon 7:11-13

Not only is she forthright here, she's become flat-out adventurous! Her attitude is, "Bungee jumping is for wimps, how 'bout you and I get naked and romp around outside together, honey?" And she doesn't suddenly turn red or cover her mouth with her hand like, "I can't believe I said that!" After taking a much-needed breath, she continues her "love monologue"[2] in a sultry Mae West voice:

> *Oh that you were like a brother to me*
> *who nursed at my mother's breasts!*
> *If I found you outside, I would kiss you,*
> *and none would despise me.*
> *I would lead you and bring you*
> *into the house of my mother—*
> *she who used to teach me.*
> *I would give you spiced wine to drink,*
> *the juice of my pomegranate.*
>
>   Song of Solomon 8:1-2

I know this part sounds really icky the first time you read it. What's the deal with her saying she wishes he were her *brother?* Yuck! But it's not as it appears; once again, this poetry is tricky to decipher. The whole brother bit has to do with her desire to be able to show affection in public.[3] If she were related to Solomon, she could hug him and kiss him on the cheek in the mall or at McDonald's and no one would flinch. But in their culture, wives

FAST FACT
Although Shulamith was using the term "the juice of my pomegranate" as an intimate euphemism, actual pomegranate juice is acclaimed for its health benefits. Nutritional reports suggest that pomegranate juice contains up to three times the total antioxidants found in green tea or red wine, as well as big doses of potassium, fiber, and vitamin C. So drink up!

weren't supposed to touch their husbands "outside." They had to wait until the doors were locked, the shades were drawn, and all the lights were dimmed before they could pounce on their men with passion!

Maturity Reveals Itself in Commitment

One of the best love stories I've read recently—apart from the Song—is the account of Dr. Robertson McQuilken and his wife, Muriel.

Dr. McQuilken is a respected academic, author, preacher, and teacher who served as the president of Columbia International University in Columbia, South Carolina, for twenty-two years. He and Muriel had a busy life with social obligations and travel on behalf of the university, as well as the joyful busyness that comes with having six grown children and several grandchildren, when she was diagnosed with Alzheimer's disease. And "normal" life came to an abrupt halt for her.

For the first few years, with the help of a caretaker, friends, and family, Dr. McQuilken continued his duties at Columbia. But Muriel's illness progressed quickly, and she became increasingly difficult to manage. Especially when he was at work. If she couldn't find him as she wandered from room to room in the house, she became agitated, even panicked. The round-trip between the McQuilken's home and his office was one mile, and some days Muriel was wily enough to dodge whoever was watching her and make the trip ten times. Dr. McQuilken talks about often taking off her shoes at night, only to find that her feet were bloody from walking to and from his office.

Because he was still young—he was in his fifties, as was she—and at the height of his career, many people urged him to put Muriel in a nursing home and focus on his job. But he never even entertained that possibility. He made the controversial decision to resign from Columbia in order to stay home and take care of her. He fed her, nursed her, and bathed her until she died in 2003. When asked about the difficulty of caring for Muriel he said, "Love takes the sting out of duty."[4]

Statistics reveal that women are more likely to "stand by their man" in times of great pain than men will stand by their wives in similar circumstances. Has this been your observation? If so, why do you think men are more prone to depart prematurely?

The best love story I've seen up close recently involves a man named Michie (pronounced "Micky") and a woman named Michele, my friend Kim's parents.

They met when Michele's date to the senior prom canceled at the last minute because of a family emergency. Paula, a girl in her Spanish class, told Michele that she should go with her brother, Michie Hill. She explained that he'd just returned home from the navy and that he really liked to dance, so he'd make a good stand-in.

Michele expressed her doubts about Paula's plan, especially since she'd never laid eyes on Michie and didn't know if he was cute or not. So Paula told her that Michie was picking her up from school that day and he could give Michele a ride home, too.

Then she could make up her mind after meeting him. Michele said she was less than impressed during that introductory drive because he had this little "Dairy Queen" curl on his forehead, like Squiggy on the *Laverne and Shirley* show. But she didn't have much of a choice if she wanted to attend her last high school prom, so she agreed to go with the silly-haired sailor.

He ended up being a *great* dancer, and two years later they got married. When I asked Michele how she would describe their relationship, she said, "Secure, satisfied, fun, not boring, trusting, and faithful." She told me that he is "her favorite person in the whole world!" Her face lights up when she talks about Michie; she says the people who know them best describe him as a lion and her as the lion tamer!

Because Kim and I are more like sisters than friends, I got to be around the *lion* and his *tamer* quite a bit over the last ten years. I watched them tease during Scrabble games, referee their eight grandkids during raucous family get-togethers, and pray for people they loved. And I had the privilege of being in their home last December when Michie danced into the arms of Jesus after an ugly fight with lung cancer. I'll never forget the way Michele held his hand and stroked his face and sang to him in the waning hours of his life. They were married for forty-two-and-a-half years.

Robertson and Muriel McQuilken and Michie and Michele Hill's marriages epitomize commitment. They meant it when they pledged their hearts to each other. Their love was greater than the distressing decline from Alzheimer's and more powerful than the insidious disease that stole Michie's breath. Their faithfulness to each other was stronger than death.

Read Romans 8:35-39. How would you paraphrase this passage? What do you think it says about God's commitment to us?

Shulamith's most compelling request in the entire Song is evocative of both couples:

> *Set me as a seal upon your heart,*
> *as a seal upon your arm,*
> *for love is strong as death,*
> *jealousy is fierce as the grave.*
> *Its flashes are flashes of fire,*
> *the very flame of the LORD.*
> *Many waters cannot quench love,*
> *neither can floods drown it.*
> *If a man offered for love*
> *all the wealth of his house,*
> *he would be utterly despised.*
>
> Song of Solomon 8:6-7

The "seal" that she speaks of here is a mark of possession, a sign of ownership. Like the waxy crest that marks an elegant envelope or the small, cursive tattoo of her husband's name my spunky friend in Texas had inked on her behind (much to his surprise), a *seal* on Solomon's arm would signify that his heart belonged to Shulamith. No matter what happened, no matter how hard life got, they were always going to stay together.

NOTES

It's the same thing God talks about regarding the *permanent inscription* of our names on His hands in Isaiah's prophecy:

> *Behold, I have engraved you on the palms of my hands; your walls are continually before me.*
> Isaiah 49:16

The significance of His pledge is that He will never leave us or forsake us. His commitment to us will never fade or fail—no matter how difficult, disappointing, or painful life may get. God's love for His beloved is infinitely greater than the deepest grave.

What "marks" you as belonging to God? How can other people tell you're *His*?

Maturity Rests in Contentment

For me, the person who most personifies contentment is my friend Linda. Linda lives in California, is turning fifty, and is still single. She's never been married, although not for lack of suitors—she's tall, blonde, slender, successful, and attractive (notice

did you know?

The phrase **many waters** in Song of Songs 8:7, goes beyond the literal meaning when read against the mythological background of this era. Both Ugarit and Mesopotamian cultures had myths about a god of order fighting with and ultimately defeating a god or goddess of chaos, who was represented by the sea or a large river. It's therefore very likely that this terminology was used to suggest mythological overtones with ancient readers. The implication is that even a quasi-supernatural force can't defeat love.[5]

that I didn't use the word "celibate," although I'm quite sure that's the case). She just hasn't met anyone she's willing to "seal the deal" with.

(In case you're wondering, it has not escaped my attention that the friends I've written about in this book—Emily, Ann, Julie, Kim, and Linda—are all beautiful on the inside as well as the outside. Thus, in an effort to improve my chances in the world of romance, I'm currently scouring the highways and byways of life in order to find a gang of extremely unattractive and unpleasant women to hang out with. When I find them, I hope to appear more appealing by comparison.)

When I asked Linda why she never seemed rest-less about marriage, she first humbly attributed it to a recent surgery saying, "I think the fact that I don't have any estrogen helps!" But that's not really it. When I pressed her, she exclaimed earnestly, "God is so good to me! I have a great job, I love my friends and my family, I get to golf whenever I want. I really enjoy my life. Plus, I can't imagine anyone loving me like God does!" Linda is *content*, satisfied with what she has,[6] because she's put all her eggs in Jesus' basket.

I'm not that mature yet. Contentment is a fickle commodity in my life. Some days I'm completely satisfied with where God has me, and some days I'm a complete whiny baby. Like the other day when I went to the ob/gyn's office for my annual check-up—surrounded by big-bellied mothers-to-be and their fidgety husbands. While I was fill-ing out the form and saw the blank for *spouse's name* next to the one for *patient's name*, I wanted to write,

"Lost, won't ask for directions," in the first and "Chopped Liver" in the next. Contentment was nowhere to be found, and I just felt like crying.

But I'm working on it. I'm learning to rest a little longer in God's divine embrace before wriggling out of it.

Read Philippians 4:11-12. Have these verses ever been an apt description for your life? What is the biggest obstacle between you and contentment?

The setting of the Song's poetic finale is like one of Norman Rockwell's canvases depicting contentment:

> *We have a little sister,*
> *and she has no breasts.*
> *What shall we do for our sister*
> *on the day when she is spoken for?*
> *If she is a wall,*
> *we will build on her a battlement of silver,*
> *but if she is a door,*
> *we will enclose her with boards of cedar.*
>
> Song of Solomon 8:8-9

It's July the fourth and Shulamith's entire dysfunctional family has come to her palace to eat barbeque and watch the fireworks. Including her brothers, the same ones who forced her to work in the vineyards until she was sunburned and sore. They're all sitting around in lawn chairs, chuckling about things that only family would find funny, and they start to tease her about being flat-chested.

Then one brother goes a little too far and teases her about whether or not she was a virgin (*but if she is a door*) when she and Solomon got married.

Shulamith is used to their adolescent humor, but she doesn't shrink back and get quiet like she used to when she lived at home. Now that she's a mature married woman, and a queen to boot, she has a quick-witted response:

> **I *was* a wall,**
> *and my breasts were like towers.*
>> Song of Solomon 8:10a (emphasis in text)

Everybody bursts out laughing at her good-natured, Queen Latifah-like boast. But then Shulamith's gaze settles on Solomon smiling at her across the patio table, and she continues more softly:

> *Then I was in his eyes*
> *as one who finds peace.*
>> Song of Solomon 8:10b

As if everyone else has suddenly vanished, her eyes rest on her beloved, and her words convey the contentment of a story that she will never tire of telling.[7]

Read Zechariah 1:14-17. What's *good* about God's jealousy in this passage?

Maturity Moves Past Red Faces

My good friend Teresa (yes, she's pretty too, and engaged!) told me recently about something that happened in a church in North Carolina, where she was booked to sing one weekend. She said the woman who taught the first graders in Sunday school came running into the sanctuary before the worship service and told the pastor that she just *had to tell* him what took place in her class a few minutes before.

She described a game she had played with her six-year-old students where she'd look at them one at a time and say in an exaggerated whisper, "I've got a secret for you." Then she'd pause, smile, and whisper with animated inflection, "*Jesus* loves you!" After which, she affectionately asked each child, "Do you have a secret to tell me?" To which they were supposed to reply, "Jesus loves you, too!"

But on the morning Teresa visited their church, the game went awry when one little boy didn't give the correct response to her question. When she asked him, "Do you have a secret to tell me?" he paused, then whispered back very seriously, "Sometimes my momma and daddy take showers together." He also happened to be the pastor's son!

I laughed hard when Teresa told me the story because I could almost imagine that well-intentioned Sunday school teacher's stunned expression. And I kept grinning long afterward, thinking, *I'm so glad that pastor and his wife weren't too prudish or embarrassed to keep that hilarious anecdote private.*

In much the same way, writing about this symbolic, erotic biblical poetry has been quite an interesting, and often humorous, journey. Sometimes I've giggled while typing. Many times I've shaken my head and smiled, desperate for God to give me wisdom beyond my earthly experience.

I hope you've had a similar tour through this

Song of all songs. I hope that, like the pastor and his wife in North Carolina, you've been able to laugh at yourself. Maybe you've recognized a prudish or prejudiced assumption that needed to be swept out of your soul. Maybe you even shook your head and smiled when you realized how you've emulated Shulamith's selfish behavior.

Ultimately I pray these pages have revealed another facet of God's heart for you, one that reflects the shimmering beauty of His perfect love and the divine intimacy our all-too-human souls are longing for. I was both encouraged and sobered when I read what Rabbi Aqiba, a noted rabbi in the first century, said about the book we've been pondering: "For all the Writings are holy, but the Song of Songs is the Holy of Holies."[8]

My sincere desire is that with all my tongue-in-cheek comments and pop-culture comparisons, I didn't tarnish this exquisitely written divine literature. Please forgive me if I offended your spiritual senses in any way. I trust God to imprint what He wills into your heart and mind, and kick everything else to a forgotten curb.

And my specific prayer for each person who reads *What Every Girl Wants* is exactly what Paul asked God regarding his friends in Colossae:

> *That you may be filled with the knowledge of his will in all spiritual wisdom and understanding, so as to walk in a manner worthy of the Lord, fully pleasing to him, bearing fruit in every good work and increasing in the knowledge of God. May you be strengthened with all power, according to his glorious might, for all endurance and patience*

*with joy, giving thanks to the Father, who has
qualified you to share in the inheritance of the
saints in light.*

Colossians 1:9-12

DVD **What was your favorite section—or image—
in the Song of Songs? What was it about this
particular part that you connected with?**

NOTES

Chapter 1: Passionately Pursued

1 V. Philips Long, "Psalms and Wisdom Literature," Lecture 2 (Covenant Theological Seminary).

2 G. Lloyd Carr, *The Song of Solomon: An Introduction and Commentary* (Downers Grove, IL: InterVarsity Press, 1984), 70.

3 Bill Arnold and Bryan Beyer, *Encountering the Old Testament: A Christian Survey* (Grand Rapids, MI: Baker Books, 1999), 331. *The MacArthur Study Bible* (Nashville, TN: Word Publishing, 1997), 941. Carr, *The Song of Solomon*, 21–35.

4 Tremper Longman, *Song of Songs* (Grand Rapids, MI: William B. Eerdmans, 2001), 21.

5 Arnold and Beyer, *Encountering the Old Testament*, 333. V. Philips Long, "Psalms and Wisdom Literature," Lecture 31 (Covenant Theological Seminary).

6 Longman, *Song of Songs*, 70.

7 Ibid., 7.

8 Richard Hess, *Song of Songs* (Grand Rapids, MI: Baker Publishing Group, 2005), 31.

9 Carr, *The Song of Solomon*, 23.

10 Longman, *Song of Songs*, 70.

11 Carr, *The Song of Solomon*, 16.

12 Jeanne Guyon, *The Song of the Bride* (Sargent, GA: The Seedsowers Christian Books Publishing House, 1990), 1.

13 Ibid., the publisher's preface.

Chapter 2: Feeling Pretty Enough

1 *Webster's Encyclopedic Unabridged Dictionary of the English Language*, New Deluxe Edition, s.v. "aseity" (San Diego, CA: Thunder Bay Press, 2001), 121.

Chapter 3: A Rooftop Romancer

1 Craig Glickman, *Solomon's Song of Love* (West Monroe, LA: Howard Publishing Company, 2004), 70.

2 Ibid., 215.

3 G. Lloyd Carr, *The Song of Solomon: An Introduction and Commentary* (Downers Grove, IL: InterVarsity Press, 1984), 90.

4 David George Moore and Daniel L. Akin; Max Anders, gen. ed., *Holman Old Testament Commentary: Ecclesiastes, Song of Songs* (Nashville, TN: Broadman & Holman Publishers, 2003), 184.

5 Carr, *The Song of Solomon*, 92.

6 Glickman, *Solomon's Song of Love*, 71.

7 Lyrics accessed October 17, 2005, at http://www.Johnmayer.com

8 Victor H. Matthews and Don C. Benjamin, *Old Testament Parallels: Laws and Stories from the Ancient Near East* (Mahwah, NJ: Paulist Press, 1997), xi–xiv.

9 Carr, *The Song of Solomon*, 93.

Chapter 4: A Huge Portion of Happy

1 *Webster's Encyclopedic Unabridged Dictionary of the English Language*, New Deluxe Edition, s.v. "leap" (San Diego, CA: Thunder Bay Press, 2001), 1095.

2 Ibid., 88.

3 Watchman Nee, *The Song of Songs: The Divine Romance Between God and Man* (Anaheim, CA: Living Stream Ministry, 1995), 34.

4 Ibid., 35.

5 G. Lloyd Carr, *The Song of Solomon: An Introduction and Commentary* (Downers Grove, IL: InterVarsity Press, 1984), 99.

Chapter 5: Lost and Found

1 G. Lloyd Carr, *The Song of Solomon: An Introduction and Commentary* (Downers Grove, IL: InterVarsity Press, 1984), 105.

2 Marney Rich Keenan, "Home Life," *The Detroit News* (June 25, 2005).

3 Craig Glickman, *Solomon's Song of Love* (West Monroe, LA: Howard Publishing Company, 2004), 87.

4 Carr, *The Song of Solomon*, 113.

Chapter 6: Too Hot to Trot

1 Victor H. Matthews and Don C. Benjamin, *Old Testament Parallels: Laws and Stories from the Ancient Near East* (Mahwah, NJ: Paulist Press, 1997), 297–298.

2 G. Lloyd Carr, *The Song of Solomon: An Introduction and Commentary* (Downers Grove, IL: InterVarsity Press, 1984), 114.

3 Ibid., 117.

Chapter 7: A Thundering Ovation

1 *Webster's Encyclopedic Unabridged Dictionary of the English Language*, New Deluxe Edition, s.v. "exegesis" (San Diego, CA: Thunder Bay Press, 2001), 677.

2 Lauren Winner, *Real Sex: The Naked Truth about Chastity* (Grand Rapids, MI: Brazos Press, 2005), 39. *Hebrew-Greek Key Word Study Bible*, Spiros Zodhiates, ed. (Chattanooga, TN: AMG Publishers, 1998), 1131, 1151, 1336, 2106.

3 Winner, *Real Sex*, 85.

4 Ibid., 85–93.

5 *Holman Old Testament Commentary: Ecclesiastes, Song of Songs*, Max Anders, gen. ed. (Nashville, TN: Broadman & Holman Publishers, 2003), 254.

6 Ibid., 254–255.

7 *Ancient Christian Commentary on Scripture: Old Testament IV—Proverbs, Ecclesiastes, Song of Solomon* (Downers Grove, IL: InterVarsity Press, 2005), 342.

Chapter 8: When Delight Turns to Drudgery

1 Tremper Longman, *Song of Songs* (Grand Rapids, MI: William B. Eerdmans, 2001), 165.

2 G. Lloyd Carr, *The Song of Solomon: An Introduction and Commentary* (Downers Grove, IL: InterVarsity Press, 1984), 130–131. Craig Glickman, "The Unity of

the Song of Solomon," ThD thesis (Dallas Theological Seminary, 1974). Craig
Glickman, *A Song for Lovers* (Downers Grove, IL: InterVarsity Press, 19760, 60–
65, 182–185.

3 Carr, *Song of Solomon*, 133.

4 Craig Glickman, *Solomon's Song of Love* (West Monroe, LA: Howard Publishing
Company, 2004), 94.

5 Michael Wilcock, *The Message of Revelation*, John R. W. Stott, ed. (Leicester,
England: InterVarsity Press, 1975), 56–57.

6 Richard Hess, *Song of Songs* (Grand Rapids, MI: Baker Publishing Group, 2005),
176.

7 Longman, *Song of Songs*, 173.

Chapter 9: Recovering the Romance

1 Tremper Longman, *Song of Songs* (Grand Rapids, MI: William B. Eerdmans,
2001), 182–183. Craig Glickman, *Solomon's Song of Love* (West Monroe, LA:
Howard Publishing Company, 2004), 111.

2. Longman, *Song of Songs*, 184.

3. *Vine's Complete Expository Dictionary of Old and New Testament Words* (Nashville:
Thomas Nelson Publishers, 1996), 185.

4 Dan Allender and Tremper Longman, *Bold Love* (Colorado Springs, CO:
NavPress Publications, 1992), 103.

5 Ibid., 103–104.

6 Edward T. Welch, *Addictions: A Banquet in the Grave* (Phillipsburg, NJ: P&R
Publishing Company, 2001), xvi.

7 www.wikipedia.com, s.v. "I Can't Get No Satisfaction," last accessed January 3,
2006.

8. *Webster's Encyclopedic Unabridged Dictionary of the English Language*, New Deluxe
Edition, s.v. "soteriology" (San Diego, CA: Thunder Bay Press, 2001), 1822.

9 *Vine's Complete Expository Dictionary*, 686.

Chapter 10: Marks of Maturity

1 Tremper Longman, *Song of Songs* (Grand Rapids, MI: William B. Eerdmans,
2001), 197.

2. Ibid., 199.

3 Richard Hess, *Song of Songs* (Grand Rapids, MI: Baker Publishing Group, 2005),
228–229.

4 Robertson McQuilken, "Living by Vows," *Christianity Today* (February 9, 2004),
found at http://www.christianitytoday.com/ct/2004/106/11.0html last accessed
November 1, 2005. Summer Bethea, "Love and Alzheimer's," *Focus on the Family*
found at http://www.family.org/fofmag/marriage/a0035108.cfm last accessed
November 1, 2005.

5 Longman, *Song of Songs*, 213–214.

6 *Webster's Encyclopedic Unabridged Dictionary of the English Language*, New Deluxe
Edition, s.v. "content" (San Diego, CA: Thunder Bay Press, 2001), 439.

7 Craig Glickman, *Solomon's Song of Love* (West Monroe, LA: Howard Publishing
Company, 2004), 158.

8 Longman, *Song of Songs*, 197.

Get ready for the next great adventure!

Holding Out for a Hero: A New Spin on Hebrews

Every woman needs a hero. Join Lisa Harper as she hits the road in search of the greatest hero of all time! You'll love this fresh new look at one of the New Testament's most inspiring books. (Book Club Discussion DVD included)

Now Available

Find out more about Lisa, her book club, travel schedule, and the *On the Road* series at www.lisaontheroad.com

To schedule Lisa for a speaking engagement, contact the Ambassador Agency at 615-379-4700 or go to www.ambassadoragency.com

Tough Love, Tender Mercies: Three Short Stops in the Minor Prophets

Join Lisa as she winds her way through the books of Hosea, Zephaniah, and Malachi with the help of some of Hollywood's most popular films. (Book Club Discussion DVD included)

Now Available

Enjoy these other great titles from Tyndale House Publishers!

Real Life. Honest Women. True Stories.

From the best-selling author of
Becoming a Woman of Excellence

Maybe God Is Right After All by Cynthia Heald

Join trusted Bible teacher Cynthia Heald as she shares the ten radical truths that have provided her wisdom at the crossroads of life and served as an anchor during times of crisis. Perfect for individual or group study, this book includes a Bible study section and guided prayer topics at the end of each chapter.

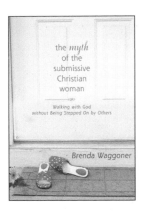

"This book will change the way you think about the issue of submission." Steve Brown

The Myth of the Submissive Christian Woman
by Brenda Waggoner

Scripture calls us to die to self but nowhere does Scripture tell us to abandon all of the wonderful God-given gifts and talents that make us who we are. Brenda Waggoner dispels the myth that biblical submission requires women to become passive in their relationships with God and others, and helps women live truthfully by putting God first in their lives and living according to his will.

Available now at a bookstore near you!

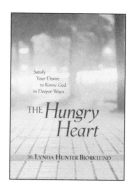

"This is the kind of woman I want to learn from!"
Kay Arthur

The Hungry Heart by Lynda Hunter Bjorklund

Everyone longs for intimacy. As Christians we know that intimacy, significance, and acceptance can be found in the arms of a loving and gracious God. Dr. Lynda Hunter Bjorklund teaches women how to get at that place with God and find the deep relationship that comes from really knowing the One who created you.

"Witty, acerbic, and genuinely entertaining!"
Publishers Weekly

Scandalous Grace by Julie Ann Barnhill

Join America's favorite guurlfriend, Julie Ann Barnhill, as she takes you on the wild and wonderful roller-coaster ride that is God's Scandalous Grace! With gutsy honesty and stories that'll have you "laughing so hard you snort," Julie reveals how you can live, day by day, in the knowledge of God's unconditional love in the midst of "loose ends."

"Today's Christian woman should be proud to be termed a 'SHE.'"
Publishers Weekly

SHE by Rebecca St. James and Lynda Hunter Bjorklund

Today's media bombard women with messages that say, "You must be beautiful, thin, sexy, successful, strong, outgoing, and independent." But who does *God* say a woman should be? Get up close and personal with Rebecca St. James and Lynda Hunter Bjorklund as they expose the lies that drive women to distraction and reveal the truth about God's plan for women's lives.